Inclusive Directions

PRAISE FOR *INCLUSIVE DIRECTIONS*

"Two things are sure: community colleges, with 50 percent of college students enrolled in them, are essential to the education of our nation, and the role of chief diversity officers on college campuses is absolutely vital. *Inclusive Directions* is focused on both of these important areas, providing practical guidance that can be adopted, adapted, and implemented on community college campuses throughout the nation and doing so in an accessible, straightforward manner." —**Marybeth Gasman**, PhD, professor; director, Penn Center for Minority-Serving Institutions, Higher Education Division, Graduate School of Education, University of Pennsylvania

"*Inclusive Directions* compels community colleges to embody the commitment to diversity and inclusion that led to the birth of the community college movement more than a century ago. Today, most community college campuses find themselves faced with the urgency of now in promoting and sustaining environments of inclusive excellence. This book provides practical, thoughtful, and strategic ways to meet this call to action. It effectively amplifies the need for the chief diversity officer and provides ways to leverage these executive-level positions so that college campuses, and the communities they serve, will be uplifted and transformed." —**Steve Pemberton**, Walgreens divisional vice president and chief diversity officer

"*Inclusive Directions* offers a vision of community college diversity and inclusion leadership at the executive level and justifies why CDO positions are so vital for success. This engaging book both shows the history of CDOs in community colleges and higher education generally and also offers a vision for how to move forward. This book is an inspiration for the aspiring CDO and useful for current CDOs." —**Jennifer DeCoste**, PhD, vice president for strategy, CREDO

"This publication could not be more timely, relevant, or necessary. As fellow practitioners and change agents at Kaleidoscope Group, we believe in the critical impact of community colleges on the society, communities, workforce, and organizational results. We also have the utmost respect for diversity and inclusion leaders who relentlessly strive for the attainment of a truly diverse and inclusive college campus, despite many roadblocks and limited resources. This book extends terrific support to all those in need of additional guidance tools as well as the affirmation of value and impact of their highly meaningful (yet not always adequately recognized) efforts. These practitioners have demonstrated the passion, vision, intellect, and heart to inspire others to embrace diversity and inclusion and necessary change." —**Doug Harris** (CEO) and **Kasia Ganko-Rodriguez** (Sr C), Kaleidoscope Group

"It is a pleasure to endorse *Inclusive Directions*. Written by three seasoned community college professionals, and intended for fellow diversity officers and others in senior community college leadership positions, this text offers proven strategies, examples, and promising practices that readers can readily adopt to more fully develop diverse campus communities with inclusive cultures. This book will be a widely cited resource and a must-read for community college leaders." —**Kenneth L. Ender**, PhD, president, William Rainey Harper College

Inclusive Directions

The Role of the Chief Diversity Officer in Community College Leadership

CLYDE WILSON PICKETT, MICHELÉ SMITH, AND JAMES A. FELTON III

Published in Partnership with the
American Association of Community Colleges

ROWMAN & LITTLEFIELD
Lanham • Boulder • New York • London

AMERICAN
ASSOCIATION OF
COMMUNITY
COLLEGES

Published in partnership with the American Association of Community Colleges

Published by Rowman & Littlefield
A wholly owned subsidary of The Rowman & Littlefield Publishing Group, Inc.
4501 Forbes Boulevard, Suite 200, Lanham, Maryland 20706
www.rowman.com

Unit A, Whitacre Mews, 26-34 Stannary Street, London SE11 4AB

British Library Cataloguing in Publication Information Available

Library of Congress Cataloging-in-Publication Data Available

ISBN 9781475833812 (cloth : alk. paper)
ISBN 9781475833829 (pbk. : alk. paper)
ISBN 9781475833843 (electronic)

♾™ The paper used in this publication meets the minimum requirements of
American National Standard for Information Sciences—Permanence of Paper
for Printed Library Materials, ANSI/NISO Z39.48-1992.

Printed in the United States of America

Contents

Foreword

Diversity and inclusion involve more than just considering race. Understanding diversity is the ability to listen effectively to and develop an understanding for different cultures, ideas, backgrounds, abilities, and so forth. Managing the convergence of these different factors and elements is both a challenge and a necessity at today's community colleges.

Diversity challenges are found in all organizations and sectors, not just higher education. But, knowing that community colleges serve the majority of minority college students in the United States, it is critical to develop a culture of inclusion. As community colleges continue to serve as open-access postsecondary institutions and a gateway to educational attainment, we must ensure that our institutions are fully versed in local, state, and national policies pertaining to access, completion, and student success issues.

It is vital that our colleges be vested in and committed to providing quality educational opportunities for all students. Community college administrators must be knowledgeable about institutional and students' rights and responsibilities. In addition, cultural competence and sensitivity to the current landscape and changes that affect our student populations are definitely skills that are required in order to be effective in this area. All college administrators should be able to articulate the importance of equity and inclusion to the broader education mission of not only their institutions but also higher education in general.

Diversity and inclusion officers cannot do it alone. The authors of this book have provided a roadmap of promising practices and practical information about the growing importance of diversity and inclusion on campus and beyond. Current and future leaders of community colleges will benefit from this work as they are called upon to lead critical conversations at their colleges and serve as role models in their communities.

Walter Bumphus
President and CEO, American Association of Community Colleges
Washington, DC

Acknowledgments

We would like to express extreme gratitude and thanks to the many people who provided support, guidance, and encouragement during the creation of this book. The encouragement and support extended helped bring this vision to reality. We would like to extend a special thanks to Alisha Carter for serving as our editor for this work. Without her skill, expertise, and, most important, her patience, this work would not have been possible.

To the many people that we have met at conferences, small-group settings, and other arenas of professional exchange that expressed an interest in the necessity of this work, we extend our sincere appreciation. We would also like to thank our colleagues, friends, and peers across our various campuses who helped us see that the work of the chief diversity officer can truly transform a community college campus for the better.

Lastly, to our families, who are our foundation and who keep us grounded in championing this effort, we extend our many thanks and undying love.

Introduction

Imagine a community college campus where the workforce resembles the student body and the campus has a distinct sense of belongingness and engagement. A campus where students feel empowered and have a strong sense of self-esteem and a true desire to learn. Imagine a community college campus where student learning is not stymied by the belief that there is only one way to learn and only one way to teach.

This description is likely familiar to those who work at Hispanic-serving institutions, historically black colleges and universities, tribal colleges and universities, or even women's colleges. Oftentimes students attending these minority-serving institutions are surrounded by professionals deeply invested in ensuring that diversity and inclusion are embedded within the fabric of the work that takes places at those institutions on a day-to-day basis. Faculty, staff, and the administration at these institutions often hold diversity and inclusion as core values that are considered essential to their success.

Now imagine if this same sense of inclusion, belongingness, and engagement could be established as the norm on any one of the more than 1,100 community college campuses in the United States. Imagine how transformative this would be for students, faculty, and staff. Imagine how transformative it would be for a nation in which the vast majority of its global workforce gets educated at community colleges. The solution is simple, and this book is designed to provide the reader with accessible ways to be on the winning side of this equation.

WHAT MATTERS NOW

Shifts in the student demographics of our communities, and subsequently our community college student bodies, have led to the emergence of chief diversity officer positions on a number of two-year college campuses. However, as an emerging position, there has not been a well-established path to the chief diversity officer (CDO) role, nor has there been agreement or clarity around the professional standards of practice. The goal of this book is to give voice to the many roles that a chief diversity officer may need to assume depending on size, demographics, and underrepresented needs for a particular community college campus.

Furthermore, the faculty and staff experience, from both highly represented and historically underrepresented groups, are impacted by the presence of diversity and a sense of inclusion on every community college campus. The ability of individual employees to adjust to the needs of an ever changing student demographic is essential if the college is expected to not only survive but also thrive in the twenty-first century.

The current landscape of our country no longer allows higher education to sit back and act as a spectator to what is occurring in current events. College students exploring their own identities and aligning with varying social identity groups has and will continue to shift the way higher education does business. Gone are the days when higher education could simply choose to be a place that imparts knowledge from books into open vessels. Those choosing careers in higher education must be prepared to address the oscillating changes occurring in society that have an immediate and direct impact on the students whom these institutions serve.

An institution's ability to effectively serve its students is directly correlated to the capability of the campus workforce to understand and respond to the needs of a diverse student body. As the landscape of community colleges changes with the shifting student demographics, it is incumbent upon higher education to adjust accordingly. These shifts have resulted in the increasing need for leadership in the area of diversity and inclusion on college campuses. Although college campuses have historically welcomed expressions of social justice and activism, they have not always been prepared for addressing the impact of such movements outside of the classroom curriculum.

Colleges, especially community colleges, need to have leadership that is ready to respond to the need for systemic change on today's campuses as community colleges prepare to serve student bodies that often share racial, ethnic, gender, religious, and socioeconomic statuses that present counternarratives to those of the faculty and staff employed at those institutions. Having a clear plan for creating meaningful campus dialogues, confronting issues of biases, and providing opportunities for education and forward movement are essential for today's community college campuses.

Failure to address the need for all campuses to have leadership represented at the helm of their diversity and inclusion agenda is to ignore the truth that strategic thinking is needed in this area. Surely an investment in issues of fiduciary responsibility, human resources, marketing, and communication would warrant an equal, if not greater, investment in issues of diversity and inclusion in today's global climate.

WHY THIS WORK IS NECESSARY

The primary benefits and features of this publication include the readability, accessibility, and utility of the book. Unlike previous books that have provided substantive literature and research arguing for the role of a CDO, this book does not aim to argue a point that the authors believe must be taken as fact. Instead, this book provides proven strategies, examples, and promising practices that readers can easily replicate at their home institution. The book will also feature the National Association of Diversity Officers in Higher Education (NADOHE) Standards of Professional Practice for Chief Diversity Officers and provide examples of initiatives that exemplify professional practices for CDOs.

Due in part to the fact that the work of chief diversity officers is new, but also due to the fact that the work is inherently complicated, both novice and seasoned practitioners have often felt ill prepared for the challenges they face in the job. Whether this is due to a lack of preparation on the part of the individual or the organization, it has left some feeling frustrated and undervalued. This often leads to confusion about the role of the chief diversity officer and confusion about the scope of the work. Those professionals holding these positions often feel isolated in their work, as if they have to carry the diversity and inclusion burden alone for the entire campus community.

As a matter of fact, it was this sense of isolation that resulted in the authors of this book connecting, collaborating, and realizing that the challenges they were facing on their individual campuses were shared by others in the field.

Through a series of meetings, conferences, and professional development opportunities, they began to exchange ideas and share best practices from their home campuses. This work led to the development and presentation of sessions on their work and their journeys. It soon became apparent that there was an audience for this work.

The authors realized that chief diversity officers and other senior campus leaders from across the nation were in need of a practical guide to navigating these often uncharted diversity and inclusion waters. This book seeks to assist both new and seasoned chief diversity officers with better defining their work and better aligning it with their institution's strategic goals. It is meant to serve as both a practical resource and a source of strength, empowerment, and validation for those negotiating diversity and inclusion challenges on their respective campuses.

AN OVERVIEW OF THE BOOK

This book is designed to be a resource tool for diversity and inclusion practitioners or those seeking to establish a diversity practitioner role on their two-year college campus. The book is meant to be a practical guide for identifying and establishing the needs and scope of the work of a CDO across varying community college settings. By making use of the NADOHE Standards of Professional Practice for Chief Diversity Officers as a framework, the authors are able to examine and clearly outline the varying roles and responsibilities as an engagement officer, a compliance officer, an employee officer, and a change agent.

The book begins with a discussion of diversity within the community college sector and explores how this work has evolved historically as it compares to business and the changing needs in the nation. The text then moves on to review the transition of the role of the chief diversity officer in the community college setting. This chapter discusses the evolution from its beginnings as a middle management role to a much-needed executive-level leadership role.

A full chapter is dedicated to a discussion of the structures and models for chief diversity officers as outlined by Williams and Wade-Golden. These models provide the first glimpse into the idea that chief diversity officers are charged with wearing many hats and that the distinct role and purpose of the CDO must be aligned properly with the campus needs and resources.

Individual chapters committed to outlining the role of the CDO as an outreach officer, an employee officer, and a compliance officer serve as the core sources of information and data for the reader. These chapters are rich with promising practices, pitfalls, and lessons learned from the authors along their journeys in their respective roles. In addition, one chapter is exclusively dedicated to the CDO as a change agent because, in all cases, it is the willingness to force change that results in the ultimate success of any chief diversity officer. Each of these chapters will also address the associated NADOHE Standards of Professional Practice for Chief Diversity Officers and key characteristics of the model.

The final chapter is dedicated to the CDO indicator questionnaire, which is specifically designed to assist readers with gaining a more complete understanding of the environment in which chief diversity officers have to operate and meet their strategic goals. In addition to the questionnaire, this chapter provides a summary of the key traits and markers inherent to a variety of CDO leader types.

The conclusion offers advice and guidance in terms of how to establish a senior-level CDO position on any community college campus in the United States. It will be very clear that in order to effectively lead in the twenty-first century, both vertical and horizontal models are needed to engage a diversity of thought and experience. However, determining which model makes sense for one's own campus will be a challenge that this book seeks to help the reader address.

Those serving in the capacity of chief diversity officer, seeking to serve in the CDO role, seeking to establish a CDO role on their campus, or currently serving in a senior-level position (for example, presidents, chancellors, provosts, vice provosts, etc.) that requires the ability to articulate the need for and advocate for diversity and inclusion initiatives and resources on community college campuses will constitute the readership for this book. It is intended to serve as a readily accessible resource for a very broad audience. It is intended to speak to the immediate needs of readers to understand the role of the CDO and to be able to establish such a position at one's institution. It is meant to serve as a catalyst in the transformation of community college campuses across the nation as they pivot to address the needs of an ever changing and growing diverse society.

1

Diversity within the Community College Context

The first community college was founded in 1901, and although early junior and community colleges primarily served as schools that prepared teachers, they were only accessible to members of financial means. However, the father of the community college movement, William Rainey Harper, envisioned an opportunity for access to all. After all, as the first president of the University of Chicago, Dr. Harper believed that higher education should be available to all members of the community, including women and members of racial and ethnic minority groups.

As businesses and communities desired to have postsecondary education institutions nearby with the expansion of an emphasis on workforce development following the Great Depression of the 1930s, the face of the community college student began to change. Additional changes in community college enrollment occurred after World War II with the introduction of the G.I. Bill. This led to a great enrollment of veterans into community colleges and introduced significant numbers of diverse populations of students into these institutions.

One of the greatest impetuses to the continued growth of community colleges in the United States was the 1947 President's Commission on Higher Education. As a result of this commission, growth in the establishment of community colleges and enrollment continued to grow rapidly. The 1960s saw the greatest amount of growth in the opening of community colleges with the

Baby Boomers returning to school for vocational, transfer, and adult education resources. By the 1970s, the rapid changes in the demographics of the
community college student resulted in a different focus on the professional
development needs for faculty in the community college as preparation for
serving diverse student populations became more important.

Additional changes in the diverse populations of community college students
was most recently seen in 2008 and 2009 during the Great Recession, when
community college enrollments spiked as many adults returned to school to
retool skills or seek opportunities to change careers. As the racial and ethnic
demographics of the student body population changed at community colleges,
the needs for addressing issues of diversity and inclusion also grew.

THE JOURNEY TOWARD DIVERSITY AND INCLUSION

Typically, the work of higher education trails behind that of industry by about
ten to fifteen years. Early diversity and inclusion initiatives were connected
to the civil rights movements of the 1960s, and many businesses that engaged
in this work were focused on ensuring that they stayed out of trouble. Most
institutions of higher education engaged in diversity and inclusion work in
the 1960s as a means of social justice as college campuses provided excellent
platforms for speaking out against disparities in society.

During the 1960s and early 1970s, a number of ethnic studies programs
became integral to the curriculum on many college campuses providing a way
to be seen and heard by many students from historically underrepresented
populations that were attempting to navigate these primarily white institutions. Unfortunately, ethnic studies programs were often seen as being for
those in marginalized groups, and members of the dominant group rarely
availed themselves of this curriculum.

As diversity and inclusion initiatives moved from being connected with
compliance due to the Equal Employment Opportunity Commission (EEOC),
business organizations came to engage in diversity and inclusion work in
accordance with affirmative action laws. As companies worked to diversify
their workforce via affirmative action, community colleges and universities
followed their lead and began implementing affirmative action practices to
assist with student diversity. Community colleges were less impacted by this
development initially, as they typically served those in their immediate com-

munity; however, their graduating students were impacted by these affirmative action practices as they transferred on to four-year institutions.

As the private sector began to embrace the notion that a diverse workforce should be less about compliance and more about true diversity in the workplace, the late 1970s and 1980s touted the promotion and advancement of minorities in many workplaces. During these times, community colleges realized a need for professional development for its faculty and staff around issues that impact students from historically underrepresented populations who were enrolling on their campuses. As more students of color enrolled on community college campuses, programs and services for these diverse populations became more commonplace.

With the creation of new programs and services for students of color, a growth in the need for minority affairs departments, expanded ethnic studies departments, and affirmative action officers was realized. Community colleges often identified senior and seasoned faculty members to hold these positions aimed at addressing issues of diversity on college campuses. Many of these positions were limited in their scope and span of control, and rarely did these positions hold senior-level cabinet prominence.

Real change requires the ability to sit at the table and be a part of the decision-making process. As business and industry came to embrace diversity and inclusion as a true means to improving business outcomes, many institutions of higher education continued to hold steady with the status quo. Cultural competency training, discussions of privilege, and an examination of the lagging progress of student success of minority students as compared to their white counterparts became the focus of discussion on many campuses. However, no real efforts to make systematic changes in processes and systems were realized.

THE EMERGENCE OF THE COMMUNITY COLLEGE CHIEF DIVERSITY OFFICER

As diversity and inclusion continue to be important issues in higher education and in greater society, so, too, is the need for the chief diversity officer role in higher education. Institutions around the country are making a concerted effort to have an architect to provide a strategic vision and direct the operations that support equity and inclusion at their institutions. While four-year institutions have traditionally been pioneer institutions of having a chief diversity officer, community colleges are now in the process of undertaking and creating roles and spaces for these professionals.

Community colleges have long been places for diversity in terms of representation of students who enjoy open access to higher education; however, having a central role, central office, or central individual to provide guidance for this diverse population has been slow to develop. Four-year institutions using the model of faculty representatives and utilizing the understanding of support for diverse populations led to the growth and maturation of the chief diversity officer roles at those institutions. As scholarship and understanding about the professional role of a chief diversity officer continue to develop with the expansion of diverse representation in the student body, chief diversity officers, now more than ever, are emerging at community colleges to provide guidance.

Tasked with providing strategic vision and direction for the endeavors that promote and support diversity and inclusion at these institutions, senior leaders and boards of trustees are working diligently to establish and provide resources and support for chief diversity officers. While this progress has been slower than their four-year institutional counterparts, it should be noted that community colleges have stood for inclusion and support of diverse populations stretching back as far as the creation of the first Black Student Union (BSU) at San Francisco State.

San Francisco State's creation of the first BSU led to the conception of black studies and was truly the genesis to position community colleges as ground zero for the creation of the chief diversity officer position. Always a place of equal access in terms of affordability and admission, community colleges have been an incubator to provide traditionally marginalized and traditionally underrepresented populations the opportunity for access and exposure to higher education.

HISTORY OF DIVERSITY AT COMMUNITY COLLEGES AND THE ROLE OF BLACK STUDENT UNIONS

To understand the current role of the chief diversity officer in higher education, we must take a trip back to 1966 and San Francisco State College. The turmoil of the nineteenth century spilled over at this institution and led to the formation of the nation's first Black Student Union. It was this event and subsequent similar events of student activism that led to the expansion of conversations around diversity and higher education institutions in the United States. This sense of activism and the demands and organization of students led to the establishment of black studies departments, the expansion of black faculty representatives at predominantly white institutions, and the birth of multicultural affairs officers at institutions around the country.

As the presence of African American students began to grow at institutions and the political turmoil of the country started to shift, so did the need to have representation to address those issues and institutions. Colleges and universities in every corner of the country began to introduce offices of support for those students. Those offices of support ultimately led to the development of the chief diversity officer role. Institutions realized they needed to have a primary point of contact to set agenda and devise strategy to advise institutions on matters of diversity and inclusion and to provide support for student populations. Therefore, in examining the role of the chief diversity officer in higher education, we have come full circle as we are now expanding the conversation to the importance of the role at the community college. After all, the birthplace of all of the political activism that gave rise to these positions started at community colleges.

EXPANSION OF DIVERSE POPULATIONS IN HIGHER EDUCATION

Just as political activism gave birth to the positions that ultimately morphed into chief diversity officer roles, so, too, did this activism expand the diverse representation of the student population in higher education. The expansion of different populations of students led to the need for support of these students. This expansion also led to the conversation about affordability and access. Communities all around the country understood the changing dynamics of whom a college education was for and that ultimately gave birth to community colleges.

These institutions were founded with the understanding that higher education was to be accessible and affordable for the masses. This basic idea underscores how, at their foundation, community colleges were in place for diverse constituents. This central theme established community colleges as the place for diverse representation. Since their inception and moving forward to an increasingly diverse society, the need for community colleges is at the forefront of being the place with the strongest presence of diverse students. A simple check of diverse populations in higher education proves without a doubt that community colleges boast the largest populations of diverse students.

EXPANSION OF DIVERSITY AND REPRESENTATION OF DIVERSITY OF COMMUNITY COLLEGES

As the expansion of diverse populations is ever present at community colleges, institutions are beginning to follow the lead of four-year institutional partners to hire or establish a community college chief diversity officer. The role of these officers is outlined in this text. Whether discussing the chief diversity officer as a change agent, as an affirmative action officer, as an architect of the diversity plan, or as the primary contact for diversifying the faculty, the chief diversity officer is emerging as a priority point of leadership for community colleges.

An examination of the work of the American Association of Community Colleges (AACC) will show a strong presence of diversity and chief diversity officers at the forefront of issues that are discussed in a contemporary context. Senior leaders at community colleges and organizations like the AACC are now looking more intuitively to these officers to set the agenda to impact policy and navigate the direction of institutions. In terms of sheer statistics, the chief diversity officer role has expanded more than tenfold in the past years at community colleges.

By 2006, the National Association of Diversity Officers in Higher Education (NADOHE) was established, and four-year institutions found a place for those working in the area of diversity and inclusion to gather and serve as supports for elevating and escalating the work of diversity and inclusion on college campuses nationwide. Although community colleges are relatively new to NADOHE, the organization understands the unique needs of two-year degree-granting institutions and the development of the NADOHE Standards of Professional Practice for Chief Diversity Officers serves as a framework to support the professional work of CDOs on college campuses in the United States.

The emergence of these positions are a direct result of the commitment of community colleges to be the primary point of access for traditionally underrepresented populations to more traditional institutions. These institutions rely on the idea that a primary point of contact must champion diverse representation, diverse perspectives, diverse faculty, and diverse ideas; therefore, the emergence of these roles has helped to shape and mold the existing scholarship around diversity in the academy. Conversely, four-year counterparts are focused on the recruitment of research-focused faculty, while community colleges are focused on tracking faculty focused on teaching. The chief diversity officer understands that it is imperative that they understand the dynamic differences and demography at their institutions as well as the differences in pedagogy and instruction.

Today, the work of diversity and inclusion on community college campuses is seen as being essential to the ability of the institution to effectively serve the community in which it resides. Just as the office of human resources, the office of financial aid, or the office of finance and administrative services are seen as commonplace on most college campuses, the office of diversity and inclusion or the chief diversity officer role must be seen as integral to the overall success of the community college. True change, authentic embracing of diversity and inclusion, and an understanding that making diversity and inclusion an essential component of the college mission and strategic change will require that more college campuses hire and empower chief diversity officers.

Whether we are talking about nontraditional populations of students, students with diagnosed disabilities, significant policy changes around Title IX, the Violence Against Women Act, or the relationship with minority, women, and disadvantaged-owned businesses, these chief diversity officers must be well versed to be senior leaders at institutions as well as community champions.

A large scope of the work of a chief diversity officer of a community college is the engagement in the external community. A feather in the cap or a tool in the toolbox of community college chief diversity officers is the relevance of being visible and vibrant in the extended community. In some instances, this visibility is the skill that brings the broader diversity of the community into the fabric of the institution. Being a community liaison allows for the opportunity to cultivate relationships with business and industry and other relevant community partners to help shape and set the direction of inclusion for the institution.

Due to the work of organizations such as NADOHE and the efforts of those who have been pioneers in the area of diversity and inclusion, some chief diversity officers hold cabinet-level positions on community college campuses. These chief diversity officers are seen as resources for students, faculty, staff, and community initiatives aimed at creating a more diverse and inclusive campus.

Although the role is ever evolving, the chief diversity officer at community colleges must be the gatekeeper of all aspects of diversity and inclusion. This includes a broad understanding of the changing landscape of diverse initiatives in the country, ever evolving legal compliance, and the pulse of the climate of the institution they serve. This person must have the ability to evoke change not only in the community but also throughout the organization to be an effective leader.

However, not all campuses have reached this pinnacle and not all employees on community college campuses embrace the notion that a diverse campus workforce is essential for positive educational outcomes for a diverse student population. This book will examine the variety of roles and responsibilities that these chief diversity officers need to fill on a variety of community college campuses.

2

Evolution of the Chief Diversity Officer

As colleges and universities transition to a society that is diversifying and increasingly intentional in examining issues of inclusion, it is vital to examine the role that diversity officers play in the context of higher education. A glimpse into the landscape of diversity professionals finds a fair number of diversity officers in the corporate world, the civic and public sector, and the nonprofit space. Their primary work is to examine equity, elevate issues surrounding inclusion, promote the business model for diversity, champion the review of equity and inclusion by senior leaders, and uncover the undercurrents of the issues related to diversity.

While noted attention and publicity has been given to these diversity officers and their work, an intentional shift and focus must be provided to diversity officers who exist, operate, and drive inclusion in the higher education arena. This chapter will examine the role of diversity professionals in the higher education context or, more specifically, the role of the chief diversity officer. Additionally, this chapter will inspect the role of these professionals and will provide a general overview of the scope of their work.

Chief diversity officers are the gatekeepers of many higher education initiatives; they serve as the primary architect for diversity initiatives at institutions of higher education, provide guidance on issues of compliance, navigate the tumultuous waters of affirmative action and affirmative action–based legislation, and help to dissect federal and state legislation that continues to shape higher education practices.

The work of a chief diversity officer is central and increasingly important to the ever changing landscape of higher education. Their tireless work entails all of these responsibilities and continues to expand as globalization increases. Current chief diversity officers find themselves in the midst of promoting equity in the opportunity for and representation of diverse student populations in the academy. Pushing hard for equitable hiring, promotion, and tenure for faculty of diverse backgrounds is an important aspect of their work. This chapter will provide an elevated view of the importance of representation for success.

Finally, this chapter will introduce the Standards of Professional Practice for Chief Diversity Officers as crafted and shepherded by the National Association of Diversity Officers in Higher Education (NADOHE). These standards represent the quintessential skill set overview for diversity officers in higher education and provide a blueprint for the execution of responsibilities for the individuals operating in a higher education context as chief diversity officers. This work is championed by noted diversity scholars Worthington, Stanley, and Lewis and is grounded in scholarship, best practice models, and research and data from practitioners and scholars around the country.

DIVERSITY PROFESSIONALS

The role of the chief diversity officer as a professional in the postsecondary space is expanding and rising in the level of prevalence and importance in American higher education. As institutions become more diverse, the importance of the chief diversity officer is central to supporting that diversification. Chief diversity officers represent the highest-ranking education official/officer to address, support, and provide guidance on institutional direction on issues of diversity, equity, and inclusion at a colleges or universities.

These chief diversity officer roles are essential to the senior leadership team at colleges and universities to bring awareness and perspective to all issues regarding inclusion. Chief diversity officers serve as navigators to inclusion for institutions by setting agenda, influencing policy, and negotiating change in the academy.

The chief diversity officer should be the primary point of contact for issues related to diversity and inclusion and should have broad responsibility to guide, support, and provide influence across the institution. More specifically, these individuals should have influence and direct partnership with institutional senior leadership teams.

The chief diversity officer position works most effectively when it is a direct report to the president/chief executive officer and a member of the cabinet/senior leadership team of the institution. Additionally, these leaders should have direct contact with the board of trustees or the appropriate governing body. They should be the first and last voice to influence policy and shape change as it relates to diversity, equity, and inclusion at their institutions.

While the chief diversity officer is the primary point of contact for influencing change and is the position archetype in terms of structure and responsibilities, it should be acknowledged that other, varying models exist to serve as the guide for diversity and inclusion in a higher education context. While these other models do exist, the most effective model has proven to be the central cabinet-level chief diversity officer.

Consequently, the ultimate goal for institutions of higher education should be for the president/chief executive officer to be the primary authority to push forward initiatives that address issues of inclusion, equity, and diversity. If the college or university president is the advocating or governing voice of reason to support inclusion initiatives, institutions have better ammunition to enact and advance their efforts to support inclusion initiatives.

Institutions that adhere to this best practice model provide their chief diversity officer, diversity leaders, and other diversity professionals the support needed to advance diversity and inclusion initiatives and the appropriate resource tools to advance change. This idea underscores the importance for diversity officers to work in concert with the institution's president/chief executive officer as they have the overall responsibility for setting agenda and prioritizing the level of importance of issues and strategic vision for these and other issues at the institution.

A review of the institutions that have been recognized for having the most significant progress in addressing issues of diversity, equity, and inclusion are those that have a president/chief executive officer at the helm pushing, supporting, and providing resources to address these important causes. This presidential dedication and commitment emphasizes the importance of diversity and inclusion as an institutional priority.

While the president/chief executive officer and chief diversity officer have defined roles in terms of supporting issues of diversity and inclusion at institutions, what are often not defined are the positions and scopes of responsibility of the other professionals that help shape, impact, and progress the agenda of diversity and inclusion at their institution. It is acknowledged that other higher education professionals are also viable layers in the work to support diversity and inclusion in higher education. Whether it is the work of student life professionals, human resources professionals, or those in academic affairs, the effort to address equity, inclusion, and diversity is a broad and flexible undertaking for most institutions.

In the contemporary context of higher education, we must understand that the role to support diversity is embedded in the job responsibilities of many and should be an aspect of all positions at the institution. Indeed, to truly support diversity and inclusion as an institution means that there is a shared and collective responsibility. To fully understand this concept is to understand that broad support for diversity and inclusion in higher education is similar to the mission to uplift student success and completion. At institutions of higher education, all employees have a role in making sure that the success of students is a priority for the institution; the ultimate goal is that all employees—from janitors to senior administrators—serve as a support to students in their academic pursuits.

This concept is the foundation for what is done in higher education. Just as academic outcomes are a priority for institutions, so, too, must be the need to support and promote diversity and to share the collective responsibility to invest in and support the work of the chief diversity officer. This effort should be a pillar similar to other priority efforts at the intuition. Making a commitment in this vein will allow for the expansion of diversity, equity, and inclusion to be prioritized for all constituents at the academy.

In addition to the work of the chief diversity officer, there are other responsible parties who help serve, support, and advocate as diversity practitioners in the academy. At various institutions, individuals serve, advocate, and work to impact change in the diversity space. These professionals include multicultural affairs officers, human resources officers, affirmative action officers, compliance officers, admissions officers, and other designated officials and employees who directly report to offices of diversity and inclusion at colleges and universities.

In many instances, the aforementioned individuals serve as de facto chief diversity officers and have the responsibility and role of supporting the institution's mission to make sure that the tenets of diversity are not only prioritized but also executed in the work of the institution to meet the needs of all its constituents. Their roles are essential in supporting diversity initiatives as they serve under the direction of the chief diversity officer. They work to advance and support the college's diversity strategic plan as the institution works to appropriately address and prioritize inclusion.

When an institution has no formally recognized chief diversity officer, these individuals must be the face, voice, and advocate for diversity at their institution. In the instances when there is no chief diversity officer and the college or university has yet to commit to a strategic leader on issues of equity and inclusion, these individuals must stand in the gap to provide guidance and support.

Such instances represent a significant challenge to the advancement of inclusion, as, in many cases, these individuals do not have the appropriate support, recognized authority, or direct power to provide oversight to push forward the agenda of diversity, equity, and inclusion. When these situations arise, individuals may feel marginalized in their roles to prioritize and advocate for diversity as a priority. Instances and situations like these in the academy are a major deterrent to the promotion of inclusion as a priority. They prevent diversity and inclusion from growing further to meet the needs of the college and those whom it serves.

In cases like this, institutions must be intentional in prioritizing the authority of these positions. They must work to elevate the priority of inclusion and work toward the transition to a model of a primary chief diversity officer. This push must also include the appropriate support and dedicated resources for diversity, equity, and inclusion initiatives at the institution. It should be expressly noted that the advocacy for a chief diversity officer is not to replace additional individuals who provide direct support for inclusion, but rather to have a central place of advocacy and direction for the work to push forward this agenda.

The chief diversity officer should, with the support of others, push forward the inclusion agenda and be the senior responsible party in place to provide guidance and support the work of other diversity practitioners. They should set the agenda that supports the work of these individuals and provide the strategic guidance for overall diversity at the institution. It is this idea and commitment to diversity and inclusion that is prioritized in the work of NADOHE's Standards of Professional Practice for Chief Diversity Officers in Higher Education.

Institutions in need of a chief diversity officer or wishing to better understand the role and responsibility for this senior leader can draw on that body of work to understand direction. This work is a lynchpin of reference and prioritizes the need, expectations, and responsibilities of these positions.

AFFIRMATIVE ACTION

The promotion of equal access to opportunity is a priority at institutions of higher education. Interwoven in the discussion about equal access is the discourse on affirmative action. Affirmative action was established to provide desired outcomes and to provide equitable opportunity for traditionally marginalized and disadvantaged populations. In the academy, two of the biggest examples of this include hiring and admissions.

While community colleges are open access points of education, it is recognized that hiring continues to be a significant issue of concern for these institutions. Whether discussing equity in terms of faculty hiring and opportunity or hiring in administration, CDOs must be attentive to the importance of providing equal opportunity and removing bias and discrimination to help populations achieve equitable opportunity.

One tool that that chief diversity officers may want to consider as a resource of assistance is using different policies supported by equal access provision for traditionally underrepresented populations. These policies will better assist different constituents at the institution with obtaining opportunity where traditional bias has manifested itself in the past. While the most readily used example of affirmative action in community colleges is that of hiring, chief diversity officers should also be intentional in looking at the business contracts of the college or university to examine where equitable opportunity and equal access is present in the business operations.

Chief diversity officers must be intentional in making sure that minority, disadvantaged, and women-owned businesses and enterprises have an equal chance and opportunity for engagement with the college or the university. Creating policies and supporting initiatives that provide fair access for the business operations of the institution further promote the equity agenda and hold institutions accountable for providing equal access in all endeavors of operations and connections with the community.

NADOHE STANDARDS

As the role of chief diversity officer becomes more preeminent and established at higher education institutions across country, one of the most essential tools of resource for a chief diversity officer are the Standards of Professional Practice for Chief Diversity Officers as developed and approved by NADOHE. Established in 2006, NADOHE is the preeminent voice for diversity officers in higher education. This organization seeks to promote a supportive and collective effort toward influencing policy, informing practice, and creating opportunities that promote diversity and inclusion in higher education.

NADOHE is at the forefront of pushing for the professionalism of the role of the chief diversity officer and providing resources for those individuals who choose this role as a career path. Certainly, the Standards of Professional Practice provide the lynchpin for the work of chief diversity officer as a resource guide for institutions to measure the success, direction, and outcomes of the chief diversity officer at their respective institutions. The Standards of Professional Practice reference critical core areas and connect with vocal groups to push forward the initiatives that underscore the importance of equity, inclusion, and diversity to the broader educational mission of higher education institutions.

Through twelve standards, this resource tool allows chief diversity officers to have a professional barometer and litmus test for their work. Regardless of whether an individual is an established chief diversity officer or is new to the position, the NADOHE Standards of Professional Practice can be a tremendous resource tool to assist individuals in the profession. Chief diversity officers can draw on the twelve standards as they execute their work and use it as a reference point to push forward policy at the institution. These twelve standards can also be shared with other constituents including cabinet, senior leadership, and other colleagues to advance the work of progressing diversity and inclusion at the institution.

3

Structures and Models of Chief Diversity Officers in Higher Education

As discussed in chapter 2, the role of the chief diversity officer is a relatively new and ever evolving position in higher education. From a structural and organizational management perspective, a chief diversity officer is an executive or senior-level officer (sometimes referred to as a deputy senior officer) who is charged with implementing a strategic vision and mission for diversity, equity, and inclusion within the academy.

While the structures and models of chief diversity officers are similar at four-year and two-year institutions, there is a significant contrast in the size, scale, and scope of these positions at the community college level. To use the old adage, "all apples are fruit, but not all fruit are apples." Senior leaders and those aspiring to become a chief diversity officer, regardless of institutional type, will want to become familiar with the various structures and models in determining what works best for them from an organizational and professional perspective.

There have arguably been a number of professionals who have assumed the role of the institutional diversity officer on college and university campuses for years without the distinction of holding a senior-level title (for example, directors of diversity and/or inclusion or multicultural affairs). While there is certainly some merit to that argument, what has typically been the case is that the fate of an institution's diversity efforts have been assigned to an individual or individuals who are primarily responsible for a particular unit or office within the institution.

Higher education institutions that place the responsibility for institutional diversity with non-senior-level professionals are practicing educational negligence. To do so places mid-manager and support staff positions in an untenable situation, as most of these positions do not have the power or authority to make decisions (either solely or in collaboration with senior leadership) on behalf of the institution—thus the need for senior-level leadership.

REPORTING STRUCTURES OF CHIEF DIVERSITY OFFICERS

Before considering the various structures and models of chief diversity officers, it is vitally important to consider to whom these positions should report and where they sit within the larger organizational structure of the institution. There are a number of existing diversity positions within the field of higher education at the curricular, co-curricular, or administrative level. These are important positions that are responsible for impacting a particular facet of the institution. However, they are not responsible for providing leadership for this work across the institution.

Chief diversity officers differ from their higher education diversity professional counterparts in that they provide a strategic vision and mission for the institution. As such, it is imperative that these positions not only sit with but also report to a senior-level official of the institution (for example, chancellor/assistant vice chancellor, president/vice president, provost/assistant provost, etc.). There are a number of reasons why chief diversity officers should report to senior-level officials. The following are just a sample of the benefits and advantages of a senior-level official reporting structure.

Keeps Diversity Efforts on the Periphery

Reporting to a senior-level official such as a chancellor or president ensures that issues of diversity, equity, and inclusion remain at the forefront of the institution. Senior-level officials who have a commitment to diversity but are not well versed in this work benefit by having an experienced and knowledgeable professional who can apply a diversity lens to every facet of the institution.

Additionally, a chief diversity officer can minimize risk while increasing opportunities for the institution by not having to report essential information up the chain of command. This results in greater levels of accountability and responsibility for the work. Further, this reporting structure allows for greater levels of trust on the part of senior-level officials who want to demonstrate control and caution in transforming the culture of the institution.

Real versus Symbolic Authority and Power

Having power and authority sends a clear message to all members of the institution that diversity is an institutional, not an individual, priority. It also gets away from placing the onus of responsibility for institutional diversity on senior-level officials who must constantly refute the notion that they are personally choosing to make diversity an institutional priority. Now, some anti-progressives will argue that senior-level officials are in fact making an individual choice by consciously deciding to advance a "diversity agenda." However, this is quite the contrary.

Senior-level officials who choose to appoint a chief diversity officer are making a bold and courageous decision to not only invest in but also establish accountability and responsibility for diversity throughout their institution. It also reinforces the notion that while there is a single point person for diversity, the work of diversity is part of everything at the institution. Thus, such a reporting structure allows a chief diversity officer to embed diversity into all facets of the institution so that it becomes an inescapable part of the culture.

Reduces Garbage Can Decision Making

Organizationally speaking, higher education can be a chaotic system in which to operate. That is, colleges and universities are made up of highly decentralized divisions, schools, departments, and other units that typically have to negotiate for resources and support. It is important that institutional diversity efforts remain a consistent part of the annual operating programs or expenses of the institution in order to achieve and maintain progress.

It is not uncommon to find individuals within a higher education institution who have a number of great ideas and initiatives with regard to diversity. However, rarely are these individuals in a position to request or propose the necessary resources in order to bring their ideas and initiatives to fruition. A chief diversity officer who reports to a senior-level official has the ability to influence the decision-making process across the institution in order to bring and keep diversity efforts at the forefront.

Collaboration with Other Senior Leaders

Collaboration with other senior leaders is probably just as important (if not more) as having authority and power. Chief diversity officers who do not have to go through several layers of permissions or approvals are able to create expediency and efficiency for the work. This also helps to establish trust and buy-in on the part of senior-level officials who may be leery or uncomfortable with peers charged with providing advice or suggestions on how to infuse diversity within their office, unit, division, and so forth.

Politics

Higher education is composed of highly complex political systems. The ability to advance institutional diversity requires executive-level and senior leaders who are adept at navigating systems, personalities, policies, procedures, and so on at every level of the institution. Chief diversity officers who report to senior officials must be able to not only develop but also enact a high level of diplomacy with internal as well as external stakeholders.

Chief diversity officers are likely to have regular interactions with the executive and extended cabinet; board of governors/trustees; employee and teacher unions; local, state, and national agencies; and the media, just to name a few. For example, recent advancements regarding the role of the chief diversity officer at the community college level has led to several meetings and discussions between community college CDOs and the American Association of Community Colleges.

By now it should become evident why it is essential for chief diversity officers to report to a senior-level official. It is not a question of whether a chief diversity officer position should report to a senior-level official, but more about setting up the position and the incumbent for success in managing and leading diversity efforts at a strategic level across the institution. Simply put, senior-level official reporting structures offer chief diversity officers the authority, credibility, influence, and opportunity to create change at every level of the institution.

VERTICAL STRUCTURES OF CHIEF DIVERSITY OFFICERS

Equally important to the reporting structure of a chief diversity officer is the institutional structures that determine what the position is responsible for and how the work will get done. Williams and Wade-Golden (2007) explored the relationship between the various functions of chief diversity officers relative to organizational structures of diversity operations within the academy. They identified a number of models to describe the top-down structures in which chief diversity officers perform functional duties and responsibilities.

The authors took into account a number of factors, including the characteristics and culture of the institution, the skill set of the individual in the position, the availability of resources (both human and financial), and the general levels of responsibility for the work as well as the position. They concluded that regardless of these factors, chief diversity officers exist within one of three models. What follows is a detailed explanation of each of the three models and their significance within the higher education landscape.

Collaborative Officer Model

The collaborative officer model is probably the most adopted model within higher education, particularly for colleges and universities that have recently established diversity, equity, and inclusion as institutional priorities. The collaborative model can best be described as an officer with limited or few human resources. Typically, the chief diversity officer will be limited to or must share administrative support with one or more areas. In some instances, they may have the ability to hire a work study or graduate student for additional support.

Collaborative diversity officers will likely be highly motivated, creative, and self-directed individuals. It is not likely that there will be a significant budget under this model. Instead, CDOs will most likely work with existing diversity programs and initiatives within one or more divisions across the institution. Also, CDOs under this model will most likely serve as a generalist for all things diversity, equity, and inclusion. At the same time, they may be considered the sole thought leader at their institution. As such, they may be in high demand as they promote the diversity enterprise and their institution at a local, national, and global level.

Advantages

Perhaps one of the most obvious advantages for chief diversity officers under the collaborative model is that they have the ability to constantly reinvent themselves. That is, they are not confined to a particular set of responsibilities, they can work with various groups of internal and external stakeholders at any given time, and they can explore endless opportunities to pursue new programs and initiatives.

Another advantage to the collaborative model is that it allows chief diversity officers the ability to develop relationships with a variety of constituents. This can be advantageous when diversity efforts are scattered across disparate areas of the institution. Thus, chief diversity officers working under the collaborative model are able to create harmony and synergy for institutional diversity by connecting people, offices, departments, and so on, who may not have otherwise been in a position or identified opportunities to work together.

Challenges

One of the most obvious challenges to the collaborative officer model is that the chief diversity officer is an island of one. Limited staffing and resources can create a very isolating and lonely environment for the chief diversity officer. Although the model provides the ability to work with different constituent groups, the CDO must constantly create opportunities on their own. Although not intentional, the position can sometimes be an afterthought in instances where the chief diversity officer is not part of the initial discussion.

Another challenge under the collaborative model is the CDO must be comfortable operating under high levels of autonomy. Of course, one should expect a certain level of autonomy in assuming a senior leadership position. However, not everyone at the senior leadership level will have the time or interest to "bounce ideas" off each other. Thus, the CDO must be confident and intentional in the leadership and decision-making process.

A final challenge under the collaborative model is that the chief diversity officer must determine what to prioritize. As previously stated, the collaborative model allows for a lot of flexibility and creativity. However, other than occasional input and feedback from the senior-level official to whom the position reports, no one is going to tell this individual what to do and when to do it. The chief diversity officers will need to be adept at prioritizing existing initiatives while capitalizing on new opportunities should they occur.

Unit-Based Model

In many ways, the unit-based model is similar to its collaborative model counterpart, in that it requires the same level of leadership and creativity in order to achieve success across the institution. However, under the unit-based model, there is usually more than one person responsible for carrying out the diversity efforts at the institution. In addition to administrative support, the institution may also have one or more deputy officers or full-time professionals with specific roles and responsibilities that contribute to the diversity enterprise.

Advantages

The major advantage of the unit-based model is that the chief diversity officer is not alone. It is not likely that the CDO will feel the same sense of organizational isolation and loneliness as the collaborative officer. Unit-based officers will appreciate having a team of like-minded and experienced individuals with whom to collaborate and bounce around ideas on a regular basis. Unit-based officers have more flexibility in their day-to-day work schedules because they are not obligated to attend every meeting, program, or event on campus or within the community.

Another advantage with the unit-based model is that it provides the chief diversity officer more stability within the structure of the organization. This model provides the CDO with increased institutional resources. Whereas the collaborative officer might sponsor a program or initiative only once, a unit-based officer can provide more frequent, sustainable programs and services over time. This can result in increased partnerships with both internal and external stakeholders on a variety of projects.

Further, the unit-based officer will most likely benefit by having a team of individuals who can provide a specific niche or set of services across the institution. For example, a unit-based officer might have a unit composed of trainers, investigators, and program managers who provide a comprehensive list of services on compliance within the diversity enterprise. Thus, under the unit-based model it would not be uncommon to find the Title IX coordinator, federal compliance officer, and ombuds officer all reporting to the chief diversity officer.

Challenges

In comparison to the collaborative model, one of the biggest challenges for the chief diversity officer is a loss of flexibility and autonomy. The unit-based officer must be accountable for their staff and the specific services within the diversity enterprise. Providing supervision and management can create additional stress and pressure on CDOs who are already operating in an arena that is grossly underrepresented and whose role is not widely accepted or understood by various members of the institution. This is not to suggest that unit-based models are not ideal; it just makes the work much more complex.

Another challenge to the unit-based model is that it limits the chief diversity officer's ability to reinvent or reimagine the diversity enterprise. Whereas there are endless opportunities to work on a variety of projects and stakeholders under the collaborative model, the unit-based officer may have a defined set of roles and responsibilities within the institution. Under this model, it is less about the level of creativity and leadership that the CDO has and more about one's level of experience and expertise leading and managing a multifaceted diversity enterprise.

A further challenge to the unit-based model is ensuring that staffing and resources operate in a vertical fashion. Although the unit-based officer has more human resources, the roles and responsibilities may be very specific to the needs of the diversity enterprise versus the needs of the institution. Unit-based officers will need to set clear expectations with their staff and institutional stakeholders in determining appropriate programs and initiatives that require participation and support from the CDO and/or their staff.

Portfolio Divisional Model

The portfolio divisional model is the most expansive of the three models. CDOs under this model will most likely have oversight responsibility for all facets of diversity within their institution. This might entail one or more functional offices or units such as federal TRIO, pre-college and recruitment programs, affirmative action and compliance, student support and educational awareness programs, diversity assessment, academic and diversity, supplier diversity, and more. Portfolio divisional models entail a significant amount of human and financial resources. Further, these models can be present at both the institutional and the system level.

Advantages

One of the biggest advantages of the portfolio divisional model is the chief diversity officer's ability to exercise higher levels of authority and responsibility across the institution. Portfolio divisional officers not only are involved but also can make decisions regarding every major facet of the institution. This can be particularly beneficial in their ability to influence major operations such as the institutional budget and resource allocations, institutional policies and procedures, hiring, and curriculum, among other areas.

Another advantage to the portfolio divisional model is that the chief diversity officer has a substantive team of people and units that operate in a vertical fashion within the organization. Thus the diversity enterprise is integrated into the organizational structure at an operational, tactical, and strategic level. It is the difference between taking diversity into account versus it being a normal activity across the organization.

Challenges

One could assume that given the array of resources and activities that fall under the portfolio divisional model that it would be easier to achieve greater levels of institutional diversity. However, there are a number of challenges that senior-level officials and chief diversity officers will need to take into account should they be interested in assuming a role under this model.

One of the biggest challenges the CDO faces is greater levels of scrutiny. This model has less to do with the work and more to do with the cost-benefit analysis of the resources dedicated to the work (which is an unfortunate challenge in and of itself). The stakes are much higher for institutions who establish a portfolio divisional model for the diversity enterprise (and so they should be if they are truly committed to doing this work). Given the significant amount of resources needed to support this model, it is vitally important that chief diversity officers are able to execute high levels of leadership and oversight management in order to meet institutional diversity goals.

Another challenge of the portfolio divisional model is that it is highly outcomes based in nature. Part of being a diversity champion is creating cultural change on an individual, community, and institutional level. However, creating change is not always easily or immediately visible. Given the significant amount of resources under this model, CDOs will be required to chart their progress and success in ways that are highly assessable and measurable. Once again, CDOs will need to justify why it is necessary for the institution to dedicate an entire division to the diversity enterprise.

As previously stated, higher education is composed of highly complex political systems. Given the portfolio divisional officer's span of control and functional level of responsibilities, it is very likely that this type of CDO will be involved in the internal and external politics of the institution on a daily basis. They must execute extremely high levels of diplomacy and tact in order to address the needs of their division and the institution. It should be expected that these CDOs will spend more time out of the office as they routinely interact with internal and external stakeholders at the institutional, county, state, federal, and national levels.

It is vitally important for senior-level officials and aspiring chief diversity officers to become familiar with the various models of vertical structures in developing or assuming a particular position. Institutional leaders as well as aspiring professionals should develop an appreciation for each of the three models in order to better understand which one suits them best. Not knowing which model to employ could potentially set up the incumbent and the institution for failure in addressing issues of diversity, equity, and inclusion at a strategic and institutional level.

POSITION AND TITLES OF CHIEF DIVERSITY OFFICERS

Relative to the reporting and vertical structures of chief diversity officers are the positions and titles that define the particular scope of work to be done. You will recall the importance of a chief diversity officer reporting to a senior-level official, as discussed earlier. Reporting to a senior-level official offers the best promise for long-term success. However, there can be a lot of variation with regard to the number and nature of senior-level officials that may exist at a particular college or university.

Determining which senior-level official a chief diversity officer position should report to is contingent upon a number of factors, including the historical and institutional culture, as well as the particular needs of the institution. It is not important to which senior-level official a chief diversity officer reports just as long as it is a senior-level official. In some cases, the position can report jointly to one or two senior-level officials. The key is ensuring that the position is able to address issues of diversity, equity, and inclusion at an institutional level.

Take, for example, a chancellor or a president whose major responsibility is to fundraise on behalf of the institution. Fundraising entails a significant amount of time on the road, meeting with existing and potential donors. In this instance, it might not make sense for the chief diversity officer to report to this position. However, if the institution has a provost who acts as the "campus CEO," it might make sense to place the chief diversity officer as a direct report under this senior-level official to support the day-to-day operations of the position and the work.

Additionally, there some instances in which the placement of a chief diversity officer is based on the particular skills and experiences of the person assuming the role. For example, an institution may want to promote a tenured professor who possesses significant diversity experience at the curricular level. As such, they were promoted to a chief diversity officer position that reports to the provost or vice president for academic affairs with a goal of advancing educational diversity throughout the institution.

Conversely, you may have a seasoned student affairs professional in multicultural affairs who has gained extensive leadership experience and is ready to do this work at the senior level. As such, they were promoted to a chief diversity officer position that reports to the associate chancellor for student affairs with a goal of advancing student diversity throughout the institution. Each position, title, and institution is unique.

Below is a list of common positions and titles of chief diversity officers in higher education. They reflect general working titles that are interchangeable with the various diversity terminologies (for example, diversity, equity, inclusion, affirmative action, compliance, multicultural, pluralism, etc.). Note: These positions reflect titles with "executive director" or above (coordinators, directors, and program managers and/or assistants are generally not considered senior-level diversity positions in higher education).

Chief diversity officer. This is a universal title used to denote an executive or senior-level diversity officer. It can be assumed by either a full-time faculty or a staff member with extensive academic, administrative, or student affairs experience. Typically, this title is used at the campus, institutional, or system level.

Special assistant to the president. This title is very similar to a chief diversity officer in that it is used to denote an executive or senior-level officer. It can also be used to denote a permanent, temporary, or rotating position and can be assumed by a faculty or staff member with extensive academic, administrative, or student affairs experience.

Associate/assistant provost. This title denotes a deputy of a senior-level official, unit, or division. Typically, if the provost oversees an academic unit or division, the deputy position will most likely be assumed by a faculty member or an administrator with extensive academic, instructional, or research experience. However, if the position oversees academic and administrative functions, the deputy position will most likely be assumed by a faculty member or an administrator with extensive academic, administrative, or student affairs experience.

Vice president, associate/assistant vice president, or associate/assistant dean. These titles denote either a senior-level official or a deputy of a senior-level official and can represent a specific role, unit, or division. Typically, this title can represent an academic or administrative unit or division. It can be assumed by a faculty or staff member with extensive academic, administrative, or student affairs experience.

Executive director. This title denotes an executive-level professional with a specific function within the enterprise such as affirmative action, compliance, Title IX, or workforce development. Typically, these positions report to a senior-level official such as the president or chancellor, as well as a vice president for administrative or human resources. These positions can be found at a campus- or system-level office of the higher education academy.

The above list demonstrates how far the chief diversity officer role has advanced within the field of higher education. Some may argue that there are advantages and disadvantages for each of the titles and positions presented. It is important to remember that "one size does not fit all." A position and title that works for one enterprise may not necessarily address the issues and needs of another enterprise.

Once again, it is more important where the position is placed (under a senior-level official) than the title and specific area of the position. What is most important is that senior-level officials and aspiring chief diversity officers become familiar with the various positions and titles currently used to describe chief diversity officers in higher education.

ARCHETYPES OF CHIEF DIVERSITY OFFICERS

Regardless of the structures, positions, and titles, there are a common set of roles and responsibilities that define the current work of all chief diversity officers in higher education. In 2014, the National Association of Diversity Officers in Higher Education (NADOHE) developed a set of twelve Standards of Professional Practice for Chief Diversity Officers. The intent of the standards was to develop a blueprint, of the various roles, functions, and responsibilities of chief diversity officers in higher education. These standards provided a great first step in operationalizing the role and the work of the chief diversity officer in higher education. The standards have also served as a useful tool in communicating to campus leaders and stakeholders what to expect from existing and newly established chief diversity officer positions.

Based on the NADOHE Standards, it can be concluded that the central work of chief diversity officers can be characterized under the following archetypes:

Community outreach and engagement officers. Community outreach and engagement officers are responsible for creating a learning and working environment that promotes and maintains a campus culture of inclusive excellence. These officers are adept at connecting internal and external resources to the needs of the institution as well as the local community. An in-depth description of the role and responsibilities of community outreach and engagement officers will be discussed in chapter 4.

Employee officers. Employee officers are responsible for holding the campus accountable for ensuring that recruitment and retention of underrepresented groups is a primary focus. Additionally, they are responsible for promoting understanding when groups are reluctant, or refuse, to interact with one another because discrimination and the need to address bias has not gone away. An in-depth description on the role and responsibilities of employee officers will be discussed in chapter 5.

Compliance officers. Compliance officers monitor, measure, and evaluate issues of compliance with regard to diversity, EEO/discrimination, equity,

VAWA, Clery, and Title IX for all members of the institution. Additionally, they develop and provide specialized training content for hearing officers/boards, investigators, campus law enforcement, and appeals officers. An in-depth description of the role and responsibilities of compliance officer will be discussed in chapter 6.

Change agent officers. Change agent officers promote an institutional culture that is fluid and proactive in addressing issues of diversity, equity, and inclusion. They often serve as a strategic liaison to all college constituents and leverage institutional/community resources when needed. An in-depth description of the role and responsibilities of change agent officers will be discussed in chapter 7.

As has been stated several times throughout this chapter, "one size does not fit all." Such is the case with chief diversity officer archetypes. It is not likely that a college or university will need to divest a significant amount of time and resources to address of all these functional responsibilities at one time, particularly if some of the responsibility is shared with other positions across the institution. It is also unrealistic to assume that a single person has the skills, background, and experience required to perform all of these responsibilities at the same time.

Take, for example, a compliance chief diversity officer. An institution desiring this type of position will likely want an individual with experience or expertise in employment law, judicial affairs, state and federal laws and regulations, as well as conflict resolution. Thus, the scope of their work may be limited to issues of workplace discrimination and harassment and developing workshops on bias, just as examples. In this instance, it is not likely that a compliance officer would address issues of academic diversity such as diversifying the curriculum.

Now, that it is not to say that the issues of academic diversity are not important. However, that may not be the priority of the institution—and certainly not one that has identified the need for a compliance chief diversity officer. It could be that the institution is already addressing academic diversity through other means such as a general education committee or a special task force charged with infusing diversity into new and existing courses. Therefore, it does not make sense to duplicate existing efforts, nor is it an appropriate role for a compliance officer.

Higher education prides itself on providing educational and organizational environments of "fit." Oftentimes, "fit" can be inferred as whether a higher education professional has the acumen and soft skills required for a particular position, department, division, and so forth. The CDO Type Indicator Questionnaire is an attempt on the part of the authors to help existing and aspiring professionals not only explore but also determine optimal environments in which aspiring and existing chief diversity officers will likely thrive and feel satisfied in their roles.

Senior-level officials will also find the CDO Type Indicator Questionnaire to be a useful resource in assessing the needs of their team as well as the institution. Senior-level officials will want to give careful consideration to determining the structures and models that best suit their leadership/management style, their temperament, and roles and responsibilities as chief executive officers. Senior-level officials will also want to consider the various levels of supervision, accountability, and responsibility they expect from these positions.

If the relationship between senior-level officials and the chief diversity officer is not well defined, it could potentially set up the position (and the employee) for failure. There is nothing worse than a senior-level official who becomes at odds with one of their direct reports. This typically occurs when there is a lack of shared vision or mutually beneficial goals within the reporting line. Thus it is vitally important that senior-level leaders consider the organizational culture, structure, and alignment of the chief diversity officer role within leadership hierarchy.

An equally important factor to consider in establishing a chief diversity officer position is ensuring that there is alignment between the roles and responsibilities of the position with the needs of the institution. It's one thing for the position to be in sync with senior-level officials. It is an entirely different thing to make sure that the role has been clearly defined for all members of the community. It will be vitally important that faculty, staff, and students view the role as one that provides a general level of advocacy and support to all.

Knowing which chief diversity officer structure and model will work best for the institution will help to minimize any perceived barriers and limitations that will be placed on the position given its hierarchy within the institution. That is, the position should be structured in a way that will ensure institutional buy-in and investment from all members of the institution. Thus it will be vitally important that the chief diversity officer be viewed as a visible and accessible leader within the internal and external community.

CONCLUSION

This chapter explored the various reporting and vertical structures, positions and titles, and models of chief diversity officers in higher education. As previously stated, there is no one best type of CDO. The type of position that an institution or an individual decides to pursue is dependent on a number of factors including skills, background, and experience of the person in the chief diversity officer role; the history, culture, and climate of the institution; and the particular needs of the institution. Chapters 4–7 will provide comprehensive examples of the various structures, positions, and models for further review and reflection.

This book includes a questionnaire (see chapter 8) in order to better understand the institutional and professional capacity for chief diversity officers in higher education. The questionnaire was developed to provide senior-level officials, as well as current and aspiring chief diversity officers, an opportunity to develop an appreciation for the various structures, roles, and environments in which chief diversity officers operate within the academy. It is highly recommended that the reader review this chapter again after completing the questionnaire.

4

Chief Diversity Officer as Community Outreach and Engagement College Officer

Making community colleges more inclusive depends in critical ways on the relationships that are fostered and sustained both within and outside the college. The connection with recruiting and retaining diverse students, staff members, and faculty is quite apparent, but such "pipelines" will not be established unless the college is actively engaged with diverse communities. Community outreach and engagement increases the value of a public community college in a variety of ways: as a trusted resource, as an ally, as an engine of economic development, and as a regional partner.

As institutions of higher education, particularly community colleges, determine the need to establish a chief diversity officer position, they must identify what the issues are that need to be addressed. Does the campus have a conceptual understanding of diversity, equity, and inclusion? Who is currently responsible for leading these efforts on campus, whether formally or informally? What is the perception of the college's diversity efforts from the perspective of the various stakeholders? These are essential questions that must be answered before deciding to hire a CDO.

Individual needs aside, the common denominator for any institutional diversity effort is to promote the American Association for Colleges and Universities framework of inclusive excellence. Inclusive excellence is the active, intentional, and ongoing engagement with diversity—in the curriculum, in the co-curriculum, and in communities (intellectual, social, cultural, geographical) with which individuals might connect—in ways that increase awareness, content knowledge, cognitive sophistication, and empathic understanding of the complex ways individuals interact within systems and institutions.

A community outreach and engagement officer is a sound option for colleges that have not had a lot of experience or success establishing a culture of inclusive excellence. Given that the primary role of a community outreach and engagement officer is to develop collaborative partnerships and create synergy and opportunity across the institution, a logical next step would be to establish an institutional foundation of support in order to sustain the diversity efforts of the college over time.

DEFINITION OF CDO AS COMMUNITY OUTREACH AND ENGAGEMENT OFFICER

Community outreach and engagement officers are campus leaders who are committed to ensuring diversity and inclusion for all members of the college community. Preparing students to think and operate in a global arena is critical to helping promote student success and the growth of the region and nation. These types of CDOs engage in collaborative and developmental strategies that seek to embed the goals and values of diversity and inclusion into every office, department, and function of the college. The core belief is that promoting diversity is everyone's responsibility.

Serendipity and decency by themselves will not realize the goal of achieving inclusive excellence. Faculty and staff must consciously approach recruitment and retention from a diversity perspective. Administrators must learn to operationalize diversity goals within their range of responsibilities. Above all, everyone must orient and train themselves by institutionalizing policies and processes. The intentional must supersede the intuitive. The CDO as community outreach and engagement officer is adept at coalescing issues of access, equity, and success in a strategic manner.

Although diversity and inclusion are the responsibility of all members of the college, it is vitally important to have a campus leader who is able to promote diversity initiatives, engage with external groups, and help to educate the college community about diversity, equity, and inclusion on a strategic and institutional level. Community outreach and engagement officers are adept at forging and leveraging relationships with a wide variety of constituency groups in support of inclusive excellence.

In environments in which individuals take action and foster innovation, they are often unaware of similar activities elsewhere in the organization. This produces an organizational culture of high innovation but low coordination. Current strategies for recruitment and retention of underrepresented groups should be reviewed and augmented, and additional innovative strategies should be developed. The role of the CDO as community outreach and engagement officer is to create more collaborative strategies and programs across the college.

In considering whether to establish a CDO as a community outreach and engagement officer, the institution must first define what it means by community outreach and engagement. Community engagement is the idea that a richer understanding of diversity enables us to work and live more effectively in our communities. Community engagement integrates the community as a core mission of the college through teaching, learning, and service while connecting the college's activities, programs, and resources to the many diverse communities across the county.

Engagement is an action-oriented activity. Such action is necessary to increase the presence of underrepresented groups in the faculty, student body, academic support staff, and administration to ensure that teaching, learning, and service provide for a diversity of thought and experience as well as to promote a welcoming and inclusive campus climate at the college.

Once a college is able to articulate how it defines community outreach and engagement, it will need to determine the functional role and areas of responsibility for the CDO. Specifically, will the scope of work be limited to members of the campus community or will the work extend locally and nationally as well? How much time is the CDO expected to be on campus, in the office, or in the community? Once again, these are essential questions that should be addressed in determining whether a community outreach and engagement officer is the best position for the institution.

Further, colleges will want to give careful consideration to the necessary staffing and resources needed to fund the diversity operation. The CDO as a community engagement officer is creative by nature. If colleges want someone who can develop synergy and a sense of community, they may only need a modest budget and an administrative support staff. However, if the college wants someone who can work collaboratively with various individuals and organizations outside of campus, then it may wish to invest in a significant budget and several professional staff members.

Furthermore, a common theme and consideration throughout this book is where to place chief diversity officers within the organizational structure of the institution. It is critical that community outreach and engagement officers serve as a member of the president or chancellor's cabinet or leadership team. This type of CDO must be able to work in an autonomous fashion in order to maintain high levels of visibility and participation both on campus and in the community. They require a senior-level official who can provide a flexible, supportive, and trustworthy environment.

From an operational perspective, the CDO as community outreach and engagement officer should serve as a chief strategist who is responsible for providing institutional leadership on diversity and inclusion to all constituencies of the college community. This work is particularly imperative as it relates to the need for community outreach and engagement officers in that the CDO must promote and harness the talent of a variety of stakeholders in order to shift institutional culture and traditional ways of thinking.

NADOHE STANDARDS RELEVANT TO CDO AS A COMMUNITY OUTREACH AND ENGAGEMENT OFFICER

NADOHE Standards of Professional Practice 2, 5, and 6 are relevant to the role of the CDO as community outreach and engagement officer. They are as follows:

NADOHE Standards of Professional Practice #2: Understands, and is able to articulate in verbal and written form, the importance of equity, inclusion, and diversity to the broader educational mission of higher education institutions.

NADOHE Standards of Professional Practice #5: Has an understanding of how curriculum development efforts may be used to advance the diversity mission of higher education institutions.

NADOHE Standards of Professional Practice #6: Has an understanding of how institutional programming can be used to enhance the diversity mission of higher education institutions for faculty, students, staff, and administrators.

Understanding how institutional programming can be used to enhance the diversity mission of higher education, helping to envision and conceptualize the diversity mission of an institution through a broad and inclusive definition of diversity, and understanding the range of evidence for educational benefits that accrue to students through diversity, inclusion, and equity are necessary characteristics for the community outreach and engagement officer.

Although the NADOHE Standards of Professional Practice do not give merit to the necessary tasks that this role needs to execute, they do validate the importance of having someone at the college function in the capacity of addressing these ongoing institutional needs. Nevertheless, the standards are useful as guideposts to help clarify and specify the scope and flexibility of the work of CDOs.

CHARACTERISTICS OF THE MODEL

The role of the chief diversity officer as a community outreach and engagement officer is the most common yet ubiquitous role of all the various CDO models in higher education. A CDO acting in this capacity must be charged with serving under the mantra of a "jack of all trades, master of none." They must have a general understanding of all facets of the college on both a macro and a micro level. This is not to say that they don't require a certain level of expertise. However, their primary role is to engage and create synergy for inclusive excellence with a broad constituency of stakeholders.

By now, it should be evident that higher education is composed of two major groups of stakeholders: internal and external. Internal stakeholders are composed of various groups of faculty staff and students. External stakeholders are composed of various entities within the local and regional community (they can exist on a national level as well). The following provides examples of the various types of stakeholders that community outreach and engagement officers are likely to encounter in their role.

Internal Stakeholders

President's Cabinet or Leadership Team

Given that the CDO is a senior-level executive of the college, it is critical that this position be able to interact and work collaboratively with the leadership of the college. Whether it be direct reports of the president or their direct peers, the CDO as community engagement and outreach officer must promote collegial and mutually beneficial relationships with major decision makers of the college. Anything less will prove detrimental to the position and the diversity efforts of the operation and the college.

College Officials

It goes without saying that every member of the institution is account-able to the officials of their institution in some way. Whether it be the board of trustees/governors/regents or members of the college foundation board, senior leaders must routinely interact with these elected or appointed members of the college. It is important that community outreach and engagement officers are able to demonstrate effective interpersonal com-munication skills as well as a certain level of diplomacy in negotiating the diversity needs of the institution.

Faculty Senate

Faculty are a central component of the academy. It is vitally important that community outreach and engagement officers foster positive relation-ships with faculty in order to infuse diversity into the academic affairs of the college. This will entail meeting regularly with the president or executive leadership of senate or council meetings and contributing to diversity-spe-cific initiatives on inclusive teaching and curriculum transformation, among others. Promoting excellence through academic programs will ensure the successful, collaborative relationships.

Employee Constituency Groups

Similar to working with faculty, community outreach and engagement officers will want to be mindful of addressing the needs and concerns of the various staff employees at the college. This is particularly important when ad-dressing issues of workplace equity for a population that is often stratified and marginalized relative to position types (for example, administrative, admin-istrative support, custodial). The CDO as a community outreach and engage-ment officer will want to offer a supportive, yet listening, ear in promoting the collective concerns of such groups.

Cultural Clubs and Student Organizations

Understanding and responding to the needs of students can be beneficial to community and outreach officers and the college as a whole. This can include addressing issues of racial bias in and out of the classroom, establishing pre-ferred name policies and gender-neutral restrooms for gender identity expres-sions, or establishing diversity-specific leadership programs for members of the Student Government Association. At all times, the CDO, as a community outreach and engagement officer, must be a highly visible and approachable leader that students feel comfortable addressing their needs and concerns with regard to diversity and inclusion.

Diversity Councils

Diversity councils serve an important role for higher education institutions as they provide an opportunity to bring issues of diversity, equity, and inclusion to the forefront. Whether leading or attending meetings, the CDO as community outreach and engagement officer will benefit by working with a broad constituency of faculty, staff, students, and, in some instances, community members who express a demonstrated commitment to promote institutional environments of inclusive excellence.

Employee Resource Groups

Unlike employee constituency groups, employee resource groups exist to address the particular needs of one or more social identity groups or a group of individuals who are committed to providing advocacy and support for one or more groups of protected classes at the college. Community outreach and engagement officers can serve as a helpful intermediary between senior leadership and the employee resource groups that are likely to exist on campus.

External Stakeholders

Four-Year Institutions

This might be an obvious choice at first. However, some community colleges do a better a job of preparing and tracking students who transfer to four-year schools more than others. Community outreach and engagement officers are uniquely positioned to develop collaborative partnerships with four-year schools. Whether they are working with like-minded faculty who are commitment to diversity or their senior-level counterparts at the four-year schools, there is a great opportunity to promote resources and initiatives that serve to increase the success of all students.

Minority-Serving Institutions

Similar to working with four-year institutions, there is also great value in working with historic black colleges and universities (HBCUs), Hispanic serving institutions (HSIs), tribal affiliated colleges, and women's colleges. These institutions provide an important educational experience for certain members of marginalized populations who may not thrive at a predominantly white institution.

Local City and County Councils

Political affiliations aside, local councils yield a lot of legislative power in making substantive changes for the constituents they serve. Community outreach and engagement officers can work with elected officials to bring issues of diversity to the forefront. Whether it be the mayor, county sheriff, or another elected official, the CDO can establish collaborative relationships with these individuals to address a number of social, cultural, economic, and other issues that impact faculty, staff, and students who work, study, and live in the local community.

Chambers of Commerce

Chambers of commerce provide a wheelhouse of influence and resources within a given community. They also provide an opportunity for growth and an innovation of ideas among leaders from different industries. Community outreach and engagement officers can capitalize on the wealth and talent that exist within their chambers to increase diversity initiatives on campus and within the region.

Local County School Boards

Quite arguably, local school boards are probably the most or second most important partner of the community college. Increasingly, there are a number of districts who have created counterpart diversity and equity officers. Community outreach and engagement officers will want to become familiar and have regular interaction with these likely counterparts in order to advance the diversity needs of the college as well as the county.

Corporations

The goals of a community college and local industry are inextricably linked. They both provide individuals with an opportunity to experience the democratic ideals of diversity, cooperation, and self-determination, among others. Similarly, corporations provide a lot of their time, money, and resources to making a difference in the communities they serve. Community outreach and engagement officers who are able to align their work with that of corporate organizations will increase opportunities for their students while promoting the benefits of corporate and social responsibility. They will also create new streams of revenue and resources in support of diversity.

Faith-Based and Community Action Organizations

Faith-based organizations have long served as the center of support and hope to underrepresented and minority communities. Similarly, community action organizations have a history of advocating on behalf of a number of social identity groups (for example, disabled, veteran, low-income, and LGBTQ populations). Whether it be the local housing authority, the department of social services, or the local ministerium, community outreach and engagement officers can play a vital role in creating mutually beneficial goals for the diverse groups in the community.

ACTIVITIES AND INITIATIVES UNDER THE MODEL

What follows are just a few examples of the types of activities that might fall under the leadership and direction of a community outreach and engagement officer.

Intergroup Dialogue

Intergroup dialogue (IGD) is a facilitated learning approach that engages participants in exploring issues of identity, inequality, and change through continuous, face-to-face meetings between people from two or more social identity groups that have a history of conflict or potential conflict. IGD is an innovative strategy to enhance participants' awareness, knowledge, and skills in relating to people who are different from them.

Unlike feel-good types of cross-group encounters that attempt to promote understanding by avoiding, masking, or overcoming conflicts, intergroup dialogue recognizes that communicating about and, if possible, working through conflict are both positive and necessary parts of the intergroup encounter. Such disagreements and conflicts can become valuable opportunities for participants to engage in significant conversations about different perspectives and tensions shaping relationships.

Community outreach and engagement officers can benefit from implementing an intergroup dialogue initiative in a variety of ways. First, dialogue is an opportunity to create spaces in which to address social conflict between one or more groups on campus. It also helps to provide education and awareness on the importance of inclusive excellence and the role of the chief diversity officer. IGD should be of particular interest to a community outreach and engagement officer as it provides endless opportunity to engage and engender the trust of various groups at the college.

Further, dialogue presents an opportunity to promote capacity building for a variety of stakeholders in order to train others to become facilitators, as well as develop and sponsor dialogues on their own. Additionally, it provides opportunities for members of the college community to develop cultural competency in their interactions and work with individuals from different racial, ethnic, and cultural backgrounds. Finally, an IGD initiative is a low-cost program that can yield significant returns for diversity efforts across the college.

Interfaith Services

An interfaith services program provides an opportunity for members of the college community to fellowship with and participate in religious and faith-based services sponsored by various religious groups and leaders at the college and in the local community. Interfaith programs refer to cooperative collaboration and interaction between people of different religious traditions and spiritual beliefs at an individual and institutional level.

Religious and spiritual life programs are common at four-year colleges and universities. These programs consist of full-time staff or contractual and volunteers, as well as national organizations (for example, Catholic Campus Ministry Association, the Hillel Foundation for Jewish Campus Life). Programs consist of weekly prayer and Bible study sessions, advising and directing inspirational choirs, hosting religious observances, holding baccalaureate services at commencement, and so forth.

Increasingly, a number of two-year community colleges are exploring the use and benefits of religious and faith-based programs and services on campus. Traditionally, these programs would fall under the leadership and direction of a professional member in student affairs. However, there are a growing number of diversity professionals and senior diversity officers who have led the charge of creating ecumenical spaces and services to address the increasing religious and spiritual groups on campus and within the local community.

Interfaith initiatives provide an opportunity for the community outreach and engagement officer to create intentional opportunities to connect the work of local faith-based leaders with the diversity operation at the college. Additionally, implementing an initiative demonstrates a commitment on the college's part to promote an environment that is supportive and inclusive of all members of the community.

The above examples are just two of the many programs and initiatives that might encompass the work of a CDO as community outreach and engagement officer. Other examples might include equity employee relations, cultural competency trainings, cultural heritage celebrations, and so forth. What separates this otherwise important work is that the CDO, and particularly the community outreach and engagement officer, is able to approach it from a strategic lens.

Suggestions for Establishing CDO as Community Outreach and Engagement Officer

If this is the first time that a senior-level official or a community college plans to establish a chief diversity officer position, a community outreach and engagement officer may be an appropriate choice. Institutions that are looking to establish these new roles typically do so in a reactionary fashion. That is, the institution plans to establish the position to address a particular crisis, or it recognizes the need to prepare the institution for the changing demographics and cultural shifts that will impact the college now as well as in the future.

The role of the CDO as community outreach and engagement officer is generic, yet broad enough that it can help set a future vision and mission for the college. It is also provides an opportunity to establish and grow the diversity operation over time. This will be particularly beneficial for institutions that have invested little to no work in the area of diversity and inclusion and are looking for an experienced leader to provide guidance and direction across the institution.

The CDO as community outreach and engagement officer must take a creative approach in helping the community college establish purposeful and meaningful connections with members of the college and local community. This approach will allow the CDO to promote an institutional environment of inclusion that reflects the needs and interests of all members of the local and regional community. The person who holds this position must be a highly energetic individual with excellent oral, written, presentation, and interpersonal communication skills. They should also demonstrate a high level of diplomacy and tact at all times.

Finally, the person that holds the position of CDO as community outreach and engagement officer should be someone that is trusted by the campus community, is knowledgeable of the cultural climate of both the campus and the county, and is able to connect and leverage community resources in order to support the diversity efforts at the institution. The person serving in this capacity must also be someone who is creative, willing to listen, collaborate, and have a good deal of comfort with ambiguity.

5

Chief Diversity Officer as Community College Employee Officer

At some point in most of people's lives, they have heard the following words while aboard an airplane: "Put your own oxygen mask on first before you start to help others." The role of the chief diversity officer (CDO) as an employee officer is designed to serve that specific purpose. Without oxygen, one loses a sense of orientation, one cannot think straight, and one certainly cannot act from a place of reason and rationality. The role of the CDO as employee officer is designed to aide a campus community in the process of getting their oxygen masks on first before trying to help others—namely, their students.

One of the realities that campuses must first come to grips with is whether their own house is in order. Does your campus understand where the issues exist among your workforce? Are you an inclusive campus? How has your campus defined diversity? In other words, who or what members of your community are underrepresented on your campus, among your workforce? If you are not sure that everyone on your campus has the same (or a very similar) understanding and definition of the needs for diversity and inclusion, then including students of color on that campus won't prove very beneficial.

This phenomenon is likened to inviting someone to your home for dinner without first checking to see if they have any food allergies or special dietary requests. If it turns out they are allergic to fish and the host has prepared an amazing meal consisting of soy-glazed salmon, the guest will surely be forced to go hungry. If the host's response to the guest's need for a special diet—one's difference—is simply that the guest should go hungry, then it is unlikely that the guest will feel welcome or included in the host's home. The work of diversity and inclusion requires that organizations act as good hosts to their employees, their students, and their community.

Roosevelt Thomas Jr. wrote a book called *Building a House for Diversity* that consists of a fable of a giraffe and an elephant. In this fable, Thomas captures the essence of what is required of the CDO as employee officer in order to be successful. The CDO as employee officer, like the giraffe in Thomas's fable, must seek ways to make every elephant, lion, tiger, and bear feel welcome and included in each institution's *house built for diversity*.

When campuses choose to take on diversity and inclusion (D&I) initiatives in response to incidents of bias and chaos on their campus without doing the challenging work of "putting on their own oxygen masks" first, they risk failing at their agendas. The CDO as employee officer has the dubious challenge of working to change the culture of a campus, and often this role comes with the ability to influence change, yet has no real authority over others for ensuring such change.

The CDO as employee officer must be strategic in their thinking and must be willing to pace themselves. The CDO has to be patient and must have the ability to engage others in the process. This work is similar to trying to turn a ship the size of the *Titanic*. One cannot just jerk the wheel and expect that the rudder will respond instantaneously with the mere force of a single person. It takes teamwork and collaboration and an acknowledgment that there really is power in numbers.

Additionally, the CDO as employee officer cannot be fully effective if the agenda for change is shaped by campus crises. Community colleges must anticipate the need to be nimble, flexible, and responsible in a day when diversity is more the norm than the exception on college campuses. In addition, the CDO as employee officer must understand that if one operates constantly in crises mode, they will fail to realize any substantial change on campus. If one is constantly putting out fires and chasing crises, one cannot possibly set a long-term vision and strategy for long-term change.

DEFINITION OF CDO AS EMPLOYEE OFFICER

The CDO as employee officer is a president's cabinet-level employee that is responsible for promotion of an understanding of diversity and inclusion and the impact it has on creating a campus environment of excellence. The employee officer CDO must lead institutional transformation while helping to create a campus climate that reflects inclusivity and equity in the workforce. Although not necessarily housed in the office of human resources, this position must collaborate on an ongoing basis with employees in human resources. Whereas the work of human resources may be focused on benefits, payroll, and compliance issues, the CDO as employee officer should be charged with ensuring that all employees have outlets for being heard, valued, and responded to in ways that acknowledge their unique needs.

From an operational perspective, the CDO as employee officer should serve as the ombudsperson for bias incident reporting and should also manage all accountability metrics for ensuring recruitment and retention of underrepresented groups on campus. This work is imperative, particularly as it relates to the need for the CDO in this capacity to promote an understanding, when groups are reluctant or refuse to interact with one another, around issues of bias, discrimination, or micro aggressions. These phenomena remain relevant in higher education today, and a failure to address them often leads to feelings of isolation and marginalization on community college campuses.

NADOHE STANDARDS RELEVANT TO CDO AS AN EMPLOYEE OFFICER

NADOHE Standards of Professional Practice 1, 4, 8, and 10 are relevant to the role of the CDO as employee officer. Helping to establish a broad definition of diversity, articulating the benefits of diversity to students, using institutional data to promote accountability, and demonstrating an understanding of the challenges faculty face in the promotion and tenure process are necessary characteristics for the person that holds the CDO role in the capacity of employee officer. Although the NADOHE Standards of Professional Practice do not give merit to the necessary tasks that this role needs to execute, they do validate the importance of having someone at the college to function in the capacity of addressing these ongoing institutional needs.

CHARACTERISTICS OF THE MODEL

The role of the chief diversity officer as an employee officer is a unique role in that it is often not the immediate focus of most two-year institutions when they enter the diversity and inclusion arena. A CDO acting in this capacity must be charged with dedicating time not only to matters of programming and student recruitment but, more important, toward making sure that there is a campus-wide understanding and appreciation of the value of diversity and inclusion on the campus.

There is a popular saying: "Failing to plan is planning to fail." This sentiment is appropriate for any campus that decides to engage in implementing diversity and inclusion initiatives for their students and the community without first examining the readiness of their workforce. In this case, failure to plan and prepare the employees for what it means to serve a diverse student body and to respond to the needs of a diverse community is synonymous with planning to fail at one's diversity and inclusion initiatives. If the workforce does not have a healthy sense of diversity and inclusion, students on that campus will most certainly feel left out and devalued.

The person who holds the position of CDO as employee officer should be someone trusted by the campus community, knowledgeable of the campus climate (its history and its current state), and invested in ensuring that a successful diversity and inclusion agenda is executed. The person serving in this capacity must be willing to listen, collaborate, and have a good deal of comfort with ambiguity. Furthermore, the person who holds this role needs to be an advocate for change and transformation on campus and that often requires demanding it of one's peers.

The role of the CDO as employee officer must recognize that this person is fundamentally responsible for being the shepherd for aiding in a culture shift on the campus. In light of the fact that most community colleges are fifty years of age or younger, they have cultures and practices that define who they are, how they operate, and how they conduct business. The strategies utilized in any given institution's history may not reflect or agree with the diversity and inclusion needs of the twenty-first-century community college. The employee who holds this position must have a clear understanding of those needs.

ACTIVITIES AND INITIATIVES UNDER THE MODEL

The task may sound daunting, but the CDO as employee officer must remember that the best way to eat an elephant is one bite at a time. The ability to be patient, strategic, and forward thinking will be necessary for success in this capacity. Development of a blueprint for success is necessary in order to make real change happen in the workforce at a community college around issues of diversity and inclusion.

Beginning with an assessment of the campus climate, preferably from an outside consultant, is important in terms of understanding the organizational culture in which one operates. Questions such as "What are the needs and desires of the workforce?"; "What do they believe to be the challenges that the campus faces?"; "Do they believe diversity and inclusion are important for the health and longevity of the institution?"; and "What or who do they believe is underrepresented on this campus?" are valuable places to start.

Additionally, ask how the employees are made to feel in the current campus climate. Do students on the campus see employees, especially faculty and administrators, that look, sound, and think like they do? Are there representatives on the campus that students can look to and gain a sense of reassurance that they do indeed belong on the campus? What efforts has the campus made to mitigate any gaps or areas of opportunity for growth that exist regarding their diversity and inclusion agenda?

Initiatives that are put in place by the CDO as employee officer must represent large-scale impact and although they may not have an immediate impact, they should represent initiatives that will outlive the person in the role. The CDO as employee officer should be less concerned with what the initiatives say about them personally and more about what the initiatives communicate about the institution to its employees, its communities, and its students. Future employees should have clarity as they enter the institution about the role, vision, and beliefs of the college around issues related to diversity and inclusion.

In the house-building process, this position will be that of pouring the foundation for the home. The CDO as employee officer won't be working with an interior decorator to select window treatments and paint swatches for the home, but instead will need to think of the work as more like that of working with an architect on the blueprints for building the house. The house for diversity on one's campus must be reflective of the needs of that specific campus. Without surveying the territory, that cannot be done effectively. Without a thoughtful and meaningful needs assessment, the plan is likely doomed to fail.

The use of a diversity and inclusion task force is advised for any community college campus seeking to gain an understanding of where their campus stands in terms of diversity and inclusion. A task force composed of members from varying employee groups across campus can provide the college with a sense of what the campus looks and feels like based on which employee group one is associated with. Are there groups on campus that experience more privilege than others? Are there groups on campus that do not feel a sense of belonging more so than other groups? Are there groups on campus that reflect the diversity you wish to have exist on the entire campus that you can use as a model for others?

Additionally, a task force can provide the campus with the opportunity to thoroughly investigate the best practices of other institutions that have had success in this area. Campuses can work to explore the most promising practices for campuses that resemble the size and demographics of their campus.

The task force will allow a campus to avail itself of the use of outside consultants that can take a look at the campus through an unbiased lens and without rose-colored glasses. The task force or self-study in the area of diversity and inclusion can be very helpful and revealing. A campus should be prepared to hear some difficult truths about the campus environment, and the campus community should be prepared to make changes to address the revelation of these truths. This process is analogous to pulling back to the curtains and revealing areas of concern that may not always align with the campus mission, vision, or core values.

REFLECTING THE NADOHE STANDARDS OF PROFESSIONAL PRACTICE

NADOHE Standards of Professional Practice #1: the ability to envision and conceptualize the diversity mission of an institution through a broad and inclusive definition of diversity.

One way to fully explore and examine the culture of the campus is to conduct a full assessment of the current culture. One tool that might be helpful for campuses is the cultural values assessment (CVA) from Innovation Solutions. This tool will allow all employees to participate in sharing valuable information about the current campus culture and the desired campus culture. Having a true sense of what it is like to be an employee of the campus is extremely important. It will be challenging to chart a new course for one's campus without a clear view of the current "state of the union."

An assessment tool that gives a campus a complete view of how the employees experience the campus culture is the best way to determine what the campus needs are in terms of diversity and inclusion. Gaining a broad definition of diversity of any community college campus and envisioning and conceptualizing a vision for the diversity and inclusion agenda can be done successfully only if the CDO as employee officer has an authentic view of the current campus climate.

Another way to gain a sense of the true climate on a community college campus is through the use of employee resource groups (ERGs). Employee resource groups have long been a staple in the private sector as a way of providing a place for affinity groups to exist while providing valuable information to the organizations of how to best serve the diverse employees working within the organization.

Institutions of higher education can also benefit from the use of employee resource groups. Members of ERGs know best what it will take to make their membership feel welcome and included on a community college campus. They can also serve as resources to the campus by providing valuable programming and services aimed at educating the campus community at large about the needs of these specific groups. In essence, ERGs can be instrumental in helping a campus develop a broad and inclusive definition of diversity, and the ERG membership can be instrumental in assisting the campus climate with a creating a vision for diversity and inclusion.

ERGs can also work in conjunction with a campus diversity and inclusion shared governance committee to ensure that campus policies and procedures properly represent the changing needs of the members of the campus workforce. Having an understanding of how to best serve and honor the employees that work on one's campus will provide the college community with great capital in terms of advancing their diversity and inclusion agenda. Often, members of shared governance committees don't represent the overall diversity of the workforce, especially those from historically underrepresented groups. By collaborating with ERGs, the campus can be sure to address the needs of all of the diverse voices on the campus. See appendix A for sample ERG guidelines and application materials.

In addition to engaging members of the campus workforce with the diversity and inclusion agenda via shared governance and ERGs, a campus community must remember that leadership from the top is essential if success is to be realized. Engaging the senior leadership in D&I education workshops and dialogues is imperative to ensure that the senior team has a clear and common definition of diversity and inclusion and a shared understanding of the need for this work to take place on a two-year college campus.

It is important not to assume that everyone on the senior team shares the same beliefs, ideas, and enthusiasm about matters of diversity and inclusion. Failure to plan in this area will inevitably lead to failure of any diversity and inclusion plans that are developed.

NADOHE Standards of Professional Practice #4: knowledge and understanding of, and ability to articulate in verbal and written form, the range of evidence for the educational benefits that accrue to students through diversity, inclusion, and equity in higher education.

As the campus diversity and inclusion agenda expands, campus communication will be vital to the success of that agenda. The CDO as employee officer will need to acquire some prime real estate on the campus internal or external webpage in order to communicate the diversity and inclusion efforts to the campus community. As the CDO works to inform colleagues about the needs of the campus and the action strategies being put in place to improve the campus climate, the CDO will want to keep all colleagues, students, and the community informed and engaged in the process.

Beyond the basic communication around initiatives being put in place, the CDO as employee officer needs to be able to clearly provide employees with the case of the cause. Being able to explain why diversity and inclusion matter to the health of the campus and the education of the students being served on the community college campus is the responsibility of not only senior leadership but also every campus employee, from the front-line staff to groundskeepers to full professors. Every employee must be able to articulate why diversity and inclusion matters to the campus community, particularly to the students. Without clarity around why campuses do what they do, any initiatives put in place will simply serve as window dressing and nothing more.

In addition to having a clear community plan surrounding the diversity and inclusion mission and vision, the CDO as employee officer will want to engage in signature programming events on the campus. Whether it be one large annual event such as a diversity symposium or a few smaller spotlight programming events, it is important to bring the campus together around events aimed at increasing diversity and inclusion awareness and action. These events provide opportunities for campus engagement and campus education. They also provide campus leadership with key opportunities to convey to their direct reports the value and commitment that the institution has made and is making to such events and initiatives.

As awareness and understanding of the importance of diversity and inclusion to student engagement and success increase, so will the importance and value of the campus diversity and inclusion initiatives. College campuses committed to diversity and inclusion must also participate in organizations that will help them to better serve their diverse students. Organizations such as the National Association of Diversity Officers in Higher Education (NADOHE), the Minority Male Community College Consortium (M2C3), the Hispanic Association of Colleges and Universities (HACU), or attendance at key conferences such as the National Conference on Race and Ethnicity (NCORE) are essential to ensuring that the institution is connected in the D&I community.

These memberships will also give the campus the unique ability to involve employees from a variety of employee groups in the work of diversity and inclusion, and therefore the burden of knowledge acquisition in the area of diversity and inclusion is not the sole responsibility of the CDO as employee officer. Many an initiative has died because it was the responsibility of a single employee. The CDO as employee officer has the distinct responsibility of ensuring that initiatives created under their leadership live on beyond their tenure in that role.

Finally, an understanding of the range of benefits to student success via having a robust diversity and inclusion agenda must be an integral part of the community college's strategic plan. Strategic plans represent college-wide planning and directions and identifies the places where financial resources will be spent. If the diversity and inclusion vision for a college campus is not reflected in the college's strategic plan, the chances that the campus community will understand, let alone embrace, the idea that student educational progress is a direct result of diversity and inclusion are extremely low. Having a place in the strategic plan sends a message to the campus community in terms of the value placed on diversity and inclusion both financially and symbolically.

NADOHE Standards of Professional Practice #8: basic knowledge of how various forms of institutional data can be used to benchmark and promote accountability for the diversity mission of higher education institutions.

There are few responsibilities that the CDO as employee officer holds that outweigh the importance of promoting accountability to the diversity mission of the institution. Accountability can be defined in a number of ways and it is recommended that the community college take a multi-pronged approach to holding the campus community accountable for work in the area of diversity and inclusion.

Numeric metrics of accountability consist of diversity scorecards and institutional effectiveness measures for assessing recruitment, hiring, and retention efforts. Nonmetric accountability measures consist of campus assessments such as bias incident reporting protocols, 360 feedback assessments, and data gained from exit interviews.

Numbers matter because they are tangible, and trend lines can be used to help all employees on campus understand where the campus is making progress in the areas of hiring, retention, promotion, and access to opportunities. Often, community college campuses will have far fewer employees from historically underrepresented populations than students from historically underrepresented populations. This often results in students being unable to see employees on campus who share their racial or ethnic backgrounds. This can increase a sense of isolation for students from marginalized groups and, left unaddressed, can result in a campus that becomes complacent with regard to diverse recruitment and retention efforts.

Once members of the campus community are held accountable for recruitment, hiring, and retention efforts, the community college can realize a substantial change in the diverse makeup of the campus workforce. This change signals to the campus community that the diversity and inclusion mission is more than words on paper, but a true commitment for the institution.

Diversity scorecards are an excellent tool for assessing the return on investment (ROI) for diversity and inclusion initiatives and provide a tangible numeric means of holding the campus community accountable for the diversity and inclusion agenda. Effective diversity scorecards are documents that are designed and developed by a number of constituents and enjoy the favor of college-wide buy-in.

Members of the campus ERGs are ideal candidates for assisting with the development of a campus diversity scorecard as the members of these groups often have clear views about areas that may be campus blind spots. These blind spots can include hiring and separation numbers, promotion and tenure numbers, and representation by historically underrepresented employees on campus search committees or as members of campus shared governance committees.

In addition to diversity scorecards, institutional effectiveness measures around hiring and retention are important for D&I accountability. Much the same way that community colleges will measure how effective they are at graduating students, helping them transfer successfully, and managing fiscally sound budgets, they should also be focused on measuring how effective they are at hiring and retaining employees from historically underrepresented populations.

To this end, the CDO as employee officer should be responsible for knowing the hiring rates and separation rates for diverse employees. This level of accountability, by division and department, can assist the college with identifying practices that are effective for assisting the college with meeting its diversity and inclusion goals. Without attention to the numbers, an institution can be allowed to function as if there are no gaps in its diversity and inclusion hiring and retention practices.

Understanding that numbers don't always tell the full story, it is important to gather data for accountability from a number of other sources in order to gain a complete picture of the campus progress in the area of diversity and inclusion. A triangulated approach involving 360 assessments for leadership, exit interviews using an outside vendor, and bias incident protocol will assist the CDO as employee officer with gaining a full picture of the campus climate.

The reality is that the 360 assessment alone, or the exit interview data in isolation, or even the bias incident reports won't tell the complete story. However, these three tools used in conjunction with one another will give the CDO as employee officer a good sense of where gaps in accountability may exist on the campus. If there are management issues, they will surely appear via bias incident reports, 360 assessments, and reports from exit interviews. Similarly, if there are bright spots in terms of management, these areas will likely be illuminated through 360 assessments and from data gained from exit interview feedback. Either way, the qualitative data gained from these sources provide information that is just as valuable to holding the campus accountable as is the quantitative data gained from diversity scorecards and other institutional effectiveness measures.

NADOHE Standards of Professional Practice #10: broadly understands the potential barriers that faculty face in the promotion and/or tenure process in the context of diversity-related professional activities (for example, teaching, research, service).

One of the most important roles that the CDO as employee officer will possess is that of understanding and combating the barriers that faculty may face in the hiring, tenure, and promotion process on a community college campus. The only way to make systemic change in the faculty ranks is to help to remove barriers, covert and overt, that prevent faculty and staff from moving up the ranks in the system. Community colleges have often been characterized as systems steeped in tradition and hidden politics. Employees from underrepresented groups are often unfamiliar with these politics and practices and sometimes find themselves left out when it comes to tenure and promotion opportunities.

Having a well-defined diverse employment recruitment plan can be the first step in taking a proactive approach to assisting faculty from underrepresented groups with navigating campus barriers to advancement. Often recruitment efforts for community colleges are haphazard and random. Ads are posted in academic journals and on academic websites without much thought to being intentional and targeted in the outreach to potential employees from diverse populations.

The CDO as employee officer must work closely with human resources and recruitment to identify sources for recruitment that will allow the campus to attract candidates from diverse backgrounds. The intentional outreach will increase the applicant pool as it relates to employees from historically underrepresented populations. An increase in the applicant pool will likely result in an increase in the hiring rates.

In conjunction with a well-defined diverse employee recruitment plan, the community college should implement cultural competence education workshops aimed at increasing awareness of unconscious bias that often seeps into the hiring process of many campus search committees. Issues of unconscious bias often result in employees from historically underrepresented groups being left out of the hiring process, and this void is detrimental not only to the applicant but also to the institution that may be missing out on talent.

The CDO as employee officer should not be expected to design these education workshops but should be expected to facilitate the delivery of these workshops to the college campus, and the CDO has the huge responsibility of gaining buy-in and ensuring participation in these workshops. This can be a substantial challenge; as the adage goes, "culture eats strategy for breakfast."

In addition to being a strategic thinker, the CDO as employee officer must find innovative ways to intentionally diversify the faculty ranks and thereby increase the number of diverse faculty that are hired, earn tenure, and earn promotions on the college campus. An increase in the number of tenured and promoted faculty of color can best be achieved by increasing the number of faculty of color in the faculty ranks. Grow Your Own programs are the best way to fill this void. Because two-year colleges are associate degree–granting institutions, it is often necessary that they implement diverse faculty fellowship programs in collaboration with their neighboring four-year universities in order to widen the diverse faculty pool.

Diverse Faculty Fellowship programs benefit the individual campus and the academy at large by providing immediate opportunities for employees from historically underrepresented backgrounds to gain coveted teaching experience in higher education. In addition to gaining teaching experience, faculty fellows are also able to gain experience working in the community college setting surrounded by mentors and coaches. This uniquely positions them to gain an understanding of how to navigate the system while gaining a chance to safely explore the merits of holding a full-time faculty position in higher education.

Most important to the CDO as employee officer is the benefit that faculty fellows provide the institution, as they provide the community college an opportunity to see how the campus is *experienced* through the eyes of someone outside of the dominant group.

SUGGESTIONS FOR ESTABLISHING CDO AS EMPLOYEE OFFICER

For all that is at stake in the plight to *build a house for diversity* on community college campuses across the country, the CDO as employee officer is a position that is most appropriate for campuses that are new to D&I work. Campuses that may not have invested in the work of diversity and inclusion, are not in crisis mode, and see diversity and inclusion as essential to the college mission and core values may want to establish a CDO as employee officer role on their campus.

Keeping in mind the importance of putting on one's own oxygen mask before helping others, the CDO as employee officer will help the community college establish a firm foundation for building other diversity and inclusion initiatives aimed at student success and community cohesiveness. A healthy community college campus is a campus that is more focused on being *ready* to fully serve the needs of a diverse student body and less focused on the students being ready to attend the community college. Completion of a campus needs assessment, identification of someone who understands the current campus climate and culture, and, most important, buy-in from the college president are essential to establishing a CDO as employee officer position on any community college campus.

6

Chief Diversity Officer as Compliance Officer

As the role the chief diversity officer at the community college continues to expand, it is important to examine some of the most essential aspects of the position and how the responsibilities associated with these roles are closely related to other essential functions at institutions of higher education. A quintessential function at any institution is the position of the primary compliance officer, who is charged with overseeing the setting of strategic direction and adherence to laws, governance, and other mandates. Compliance officers are a primary point of authority regarding the legislation institutions have to adhere to and these roles function to develop, support, and enforce policies at institutions.

The priority for a chief diversity officer serving as the compliance officer or supervisor of the compliance officer is to identify and provide direct support for critical issues facing the institution. Diversity and inclusion initiatives are often challenged in higher education; the aforementioned model provides an interesting landscape in which direct oversight of the compliance program at an institution raises the visibility of these positions and provides a greater validity for the need of these positions. While diversity and inclusion initiatives are often something institutions *should do*, compliance initiatives *must be* implemented for institutions to continue receiving governmental funding and logistical operation of day-to-day operations.

Central to the role of the position of the chief diversity officer serving to support compliance is the need for a guiding framework or roadmap to provide assistance with oversight and responsibility. While each institution has its own idea for the roles and responsibility for a compliance officer, the National Association of Diversity Officers in Higher Education (NADOHE) helps provide information and guidance around the core responsibilities for chief diversity officers and those working to provide guidance in the compliance arena. The NADOHE Standards of Professional Practice provide three anchoring standards that provide a foundation for the work of compliance officers.

NADOHE STANDARDS OF PROFESSIONAL PRACTICE

The NADOHE Standards of Professional Practice numbers 7, 11, and 12 all provide support for the expectation of job roles, competency understanding, and expectations for chief diversity officers working to provide support with compliance. These standards provide competency guidance on some of the required content knowledge for those chief diversity officers who work to provide institutional leadership in this area. Additionally, these standards provide information on the expectations and responsibilities of those professionals who work to serve institutions as compliance officers.

NADOHE Standard 7

Central to the role of providing support for compliance is the necessity for having an understanding and capacity to respond to incidents of bias at one's institution. Chief diversity officers must have an understanding of the proper procedures to respond to bias-related incidents at the college where they are employed. This understanding involves the procedural knowledge to process and execute investigations and to respond to complaints. Additionally, chief diversity officers must use their knowledge and skill to provide guidance to relevant and involved staff and faculty directly connected to incidents of bias.

NADOHE Standard 11

The importance of compliance officers having a direct insight and understanding of issues of nondiscrimination, access, and equity in higher education is a necessity. NADOHE Standard 11 provides information on the appropriate historical and current knowledge necessary for chief diversity officers to provide guidance around compliance.

As part of the role and responsibility, chief diversity officers must have the appropriate understanding of knowledge as it relates to the history of access and equity in higher education. Chief diversity officers must be well versed on the appropriate information of laws, policies, and regulations as it relates to the institutional responsibilities for which they have oversight. This core competency is essential as these individuals guide the institution's oversight and policy adherence to relevant laws and regulations that impact equity.

NADOHE Standard 12

Chief diversity officers who provide support for guidance in the compliance area must have direct knowledge and understanding of laws, regulations, and policies that impact inclusion in higher education. These professionals must be the institution's guide for advancing adherence to meet the expectations of federal, state, and local law mandates. They must provide guidance for the institution including the senior leadership team and the president around the goals of advancing diversity and inclusion with respect to laws that support and advance inclusion.

As such, chief diversity officers who support compliance directly must remain informed and educated on the various laws and regulations that support compliance. They must be intentional in obtaining relevant and timely information and should be the primary distributor of this information to the college community.

FEDERAL MANDATES

In certain institutions where the role of the chief diversity officer and diversity and inclusion initiatives are questioned, a direct tie to the responsibility for compliance and appropriate legal oversight further underscores the value, expertise, and importance of this role. Indeed, chief diversity officers who provide guidance and oversight of compliance are critical to the operations of the senior leadership team as they navigate through difficult waters in certain legal issues and help the directives of the college in relation to law and practice. Chief diversity officers who provide compliance guidance oversee some of these federal mandates:

- Title IX of the Education Amendments of 1972
- Violence Against Women Act
- Executive Order 11246
- Rehabilitation Act of 1973
- Vietnam Era Veterans Readjustment Assistance Act of 1974
- Jeanne Clery Act of 1990 and subsequent Campus SaVE Act
- Titles VI and VII of the Civil Rights Act of 1964
- Sections 503 and 504 of the Rehabilitation Act of 1973
- The Age Discrimination Act of 1975
- Title II of the Americans with Disabilities Act of 1990
- Health Insurance Portability and Accountability Act (HIPAA) and the Health Information Technology for Economic and Clinical Health Act (HI-TECH) for those institutions with health care facilities, and several others as it relates to federal laws and laws governing particular states

As the importance of compliance and compliance-related guidance becomes more intense and a more compelling issue for higher education institutions, having the chief diversity officer serve in this role is of significant value. This value is directly related to expressing the level of importance of these roles and because it provides greater insight into the skill and ability of these professionals in higher education.

Indeed, for those who question the legitimacy and importance of the chief diversity officer, responses are directly tied to the outcomes of the compliance program they oversee. While the individuals who question the role of the chief diversity officer are oblivious to the importance of diversity and inclusion at institutions and society in general, they cannot question the level of legal ramifications that will occur when the compliance program is not implemented properly.

It is noted that while institutions allocate significantly for other values related to chief diversity officers, it is also critical to have the necessary skills and competencies to address compliance. To give a broader understanding of the role of the chief diversity officer in providing oversight of compliance, the various aspects of the position will be reviewed in this chapter. These aspects represent some of the more crucial components of the position and the necessary skills that a chief diversity officer must possess to fulfill the obligations related to oversight of compliance.

TITLE IX OF THE EDUCATION AMENDMENTS OF 1972

Title IX of the Education Amendments of 1972 established that "no person in the United States shall, on the basis of sex, be excluded from participation in, be denied the benefits of, or be subjected to discrimination under any education program or activity receiving Federal financial assistance." The recent climate in higher education has been transfixed on Title IX and, more specifically, the issues relating to sexual violence and sexual violence awareness and prevention.

As these issues have moved to the forefront under the administration of President Barack Obama, colleges and universities have had to work diligently to make sure they address issues related to sexual violence in an expedient manner. In a very public fashion, a number of institutions have been pushed into the public eye for their inability to deal with issues of and relating to sexual violence.

Several institutions have found Title IX compliance to be cumbersome and have been slow to respond to and implement the guidance issued by the federal government. The Dear Colleague Letter, dated April 4, 2011, and subsequent guidance to provide clarity, provided institutions with specific guidance on how to address sexual violence in college settings. As colleges and universities worked to identify a landing space and responsible institutional area for these issues, the diversity office, overseen by the chief diversity officer, emerged as the primary place of responsibility and many chief diversity officers found themselves minted as the Title IX coordinator for the institution.

Chief diversity officers at various institutions around the country now found themselves providing guidance to other designated individuals who oversaw the previous Title IX compliance program as it relates to athletics, while implementing the new regulations. When President Obama signed the Violence Against Women Reauthorization Act of 2013, an additional area of responsibility for chief diversity officers emerged to coordinate compliance with the Jeanne Clery Act of 1990 as the Campus SaVE Act (implemented by the Violence Against Women Act) amended Clery to merge it and Title IX together.

This new merging of federal legislation increased institutional response as it relates to domestic violence, dating violence, sexual assault, and stalking. The chief diversity officer in this capacity provides significant guidance and information for the development of the annual security report that all institutions must publish by October 1 of each year.

Those individuals who provide this guidance must work in concert with campus security and other constituents at the institution to make sure there is fair representation and communication around information in this area. Additionally, these individuals must work directly with student life professionals to ensure there is appropriate training and education in relation to sexual violence awareness and prevention at the institution. Chief diversity officers who address these concerns must be the content area expert to inform the student orientation process to ensure new students are aware of their rights and responsibilities at the institution.

CAMPUS SECURITY CONNECTION/RESPONSE TEAMS

As chief diversity officers work in the space to provide guidance and oversight of compliance, a critical tool of benefit for the officers is a direct working relationship with the institution's campus police or security staff and oversight or participation in a college-wide response team. Access to these tools provide an opportunity for chief diversity officers who support compliance to quickly connect with key stakeholders who are informed and connected to the day-to-day operations of the college. These connections can assist with providing expedient and relevant information on upcoming issues of concern, as well as timely updates on the progression of response to action taken to remedy compliance barriers at the institution.

CONNECTION TO CAMPUS SECURITY

Chief diversity officers who function as or provide oversight to compliance must have a direct line of access and a close working relationship with college police and/or campus security staff. The campus police and/or security staff provide front-line support and protection to the institution's faculty, staff, students, and its daily operations. As these individuals are in the front line of service, they have direct information and insight into ongoing and potential threats to legal compliance issues. Whether it is direct knowledge of potential incidents of harassment or a response to immediate threats at the institution, the college's police and security staff are the operational unit to provide immediate response to concerns at the institution.

As such, these units must directly inform and involve compliance officers in the happenings of the institutions. An essential component of chief diversity officers who directly support compliance is to have a direct line of communication with the responsible party who oversees or provides guidance to campus security/safety. It is advised that these individuals have a standing meeting so as to keep each party informed on upcoming issues or concerns relative to compliance as well as emerging legal mandates. Every effort should be made to cultivate open communication and dialogue.

In addition to the one-to-one relationships between the chief diversity officer and the responsible party/parties for campus safety/security should be a direct relationship regarding diversity and sensitivity training for campus police and/or security officers and staff. Chief diversity officers who provide oversight of compliance must work with these units to ensure that cultural sensitivity and awareness are a priority.

These officers should work with the aforementioned units to coordinate ongoing cultural competency training to help prepare these individuals with the appropriate tools to respond and engage with diverse constituents. This training must be informative on the nuances of cultural difference and should be influenced by the broad diverse representation at the respective institution of service and the external community.

In situations where there have been historical concerns around trust and support with certain populations of constituents at the institution or in the community, the chief diversity officer must provide additional training and awareness around cultural sensitivity to support these groups.

The chief diversity officer must work with the multiple constituent bases to promote broader communication and awareness on behalf of the institution. They should work to inform the campus police/security staff of any ongoing concerns and work to diffuse them. The chief diversity officer should function as the *go between* to help promote better communication between the campus police/safety staff and the group to promote more transparency and trust and work to promote future positive interactions in response.

TAKING ACTION

Institutions must be intentional in action and focus on working to take action on incidents of bias. They must have a dedicated team of responders that support the mission of the compliance officer to work proactively to address bias-related incidents and concerns. Thus the creation of an incident/bias response team is an essential tool for chief diversity officers to help support the mission of compliance oversight.

Composed of various leaders throughout the college and convened by the chief diversity officer, these teams are the primary body to respond to incidents of bias and harassment. They work as a council to address institutional concerns in the area of bias or harassment. These bodies should meet at least bi-weekly to check in and review current incidents of bias or harassment at the institution. The incidents that are shared at these council meeting help inform the compliance officer of the contemporary concerns at the institution and further develop the areas of concern.

Chief diversity officers who provide oversight of compliance should use this information as a tool to guide the institution's response to certain areas of harassment and bias, as well as a resource to inform training and education for the college. This council should also be used as a mechanism to inform the broader institutional leadership team on current incidents of bias and the need for appropriate response and training. The incident of bias response team should be composed of the following:

- Chief diversity officer/compliance officer: primary convener
- Campus police/security chief
- Vice president of student affairs/dean of students
- Academic dean
- General counsel
- Faculty representative
- Staff representative

Just as training and education must be offered to students, chief diversity officers who work in compliance must also provide the same information and training to employees around the issues of sexual violence prevention and awareness. This training program must work in concert with the already established training program regarding unlawful harassment and discrimination that employers are required to provide via the Equal Employment Opportunity Commission (EEOC).

As federal agencies continue to implement new regulations for employers and higher education institutions, a thorough examination must take place to ensure proposer support and adherence to each without a duplication of efforts that may confuse trainees. Proper attention must be given to provide the appropriate level of education and information for all employees. In addition to the compliance officer, this must include employees who serve as campus security authorities, those who serve as supervisors, and employees designated to ensure confidentiality in support and service to others. A clear designation of responsibility is an important component to promote compliance. It should be noted that confusion regarding these roles and responsibilities can have the largest impact on compliance because individuals may unknowingly be noncompliant with the directives set forth by the federal regulatory bodies.

THE CHIEF DIVERSITY OFFICER AS THE EQUAL EMPLOYMENT OPPORTUNITY (EEO) OFFICER

In examining the role of the chief diversity officer and their work in the area of compliance, serving as the EEO officer and addressing legislation like Titles VI and VII of the Civil Rights Act of 1964 and investigating complaints of violations of them is a primary responsibility. Chief diversity officers must be intentional in examining issues of unlawful harassment and discrimination based on a protected classification. While these protected classifications may vary from state to state, a comprehensive nondiscrimination program addresses (at the very least):

- Race
- Ethnicity
- Color
- Religion
- National origin
- Ancestry or place of birth
- Sex
- Gender identity or expression
- Perceived gender identity
- Sexual orientation
- Disability
- Use of a service animal due to disability
- Marital status
- Familial status
- Genetic information

- Veteran status
- Age
- Any other protected classification as designated by law

In this role, the chief diversity officer is tasked with legal compliance to ensure every education and employment program it operates is free from unlawful discrimination and harassment. This includes proper dissemination and training of the nondiscrimination policies/procedures to all community members, inclusion of the nondiscrimination statement on each publication, investigating complaints of unlawful discrimination and harassment, and assisting the institution with remedying the effects of any unlawful harassment or discrimination that occurs. This also includes serving as an institutional representative in court or during arbitration. These responsibilities require the chief diversity officer to be the leading content expert on these matters and serve in a human resources capacity.

The chief diversity officer must also be a key stakeholder in the hiring operations at institutions, especially those who are public. Hiring initiatives should ensure that each position filled was done so equitably and that the best possible candidate was selected. This requires the chief diversity officer to develop hiring procedures in concert with human resources and ensure that each search committee has diverse representation. Initiatives as such ensure that diversity and inclusion are a priority at the institution and also that, if challenged, the search process will prove to be free from unlawful discrimination.

While many institutions separate the role of the EEO officer from the chief diversity officer's responsibilities, special attention should be paid to the institutions whose chief diversity officer serves as the EEO officer. These individuals have enhanced responsibility to protect the institution from legal liability and must work as a liaison between many different areas on campus. A strong working relationship with the human resources office must be established in order to level the appropriate response to complaints of unlawful discrimination or harassment.

These individuals must also work closely with general counsel in instances that an outside complaint is lodged against the institution. The chief diversity officer in these instances has a significant role in the organization, and the level of respect and resources this individual receives must match those responsibilities.

The focus of this work blends well with the overall mission to promote inclusion as a priority for the institution. In working to curtail the issues of unlawful harassment and discrimination, chief diversity officers have helped to establish a culture and climate at the institution that respect the rights of all. Working to address unlawful harassment and discrimination further allows the chief diversity officer to promote an institutional climate that is positive and receptive of embracing inclusion as a priority area as these two ideas work in concert and complement each other.

THE CHIEF DIVERSITY OFFICER AND SUPPORTIVE SERVICES FOR DISABILITIES

Another area of oversight under the umbrella of compliance is the responsibility of disability accommodations and compliance and the oversight of supportive services at the institution for both students and staff. Chief diversity officers must guide institutions in making appropriate decisions with regard to reasonable disability accommodations for students and employees.

This responsibility requires the chief diversity officer to establish a close working relationship with several constituents in the institution including, but not limited to, the provost, deans, supportive service directors, human resources, and facilities management departments. Clear policy development must occur so that compliance with reasonable accommodations, unlawful harassment and discrimination issues, universal design, and academic issues can occur in a safe and supportive environment for those needing to utilize the policies. This requires institutions to provide the chief diversity officer with the authority to ensure that these programs are implemented effectively.

As diversity is an overarching term that essentially means anything that is different, institutions must make certain they are providing proper attention in making the institution accessible and accommodating for all. To this end, institutions that utilize the chief diversity officer as the chief compliance officer have an enhanced knowledge and understanding of how each impacts and strengthens the other.

7

Chief Diversity Officer as Change Agent

Undoubtedly, the chief diversity officer at institutions of higher education wears many hats of responsibility and fulfills a number of roles in the scope of duties at the organization. One of the most essential roles of the chief diversity officer is being a catalyst for change to ensure equal opportunity for all. This crucial role as a "change agent" allows the chief diversity officer to provide oversight that promotes an environment that is receptive to issues of inclusion and one that is intentional in addressing equity and inclusion.

Whether it is working proactively to address issues of organizational climate; attending to issues of faculty representation and buy-in; promoting the attraction, retention, and involvement of a diverse employee and student body; or working to impact policies, procedures, and compliance at the institution, the role of change agent is an indispensable expectation for those individuals serving as chief diversity officers.

While the scope of responsibility of serving as a change agent can take the form of various designations, the importance of proactive leadership is nonnegotiable. The constantly changing current of issues at the academy requires that chief diversity officers be proactive advocates for holistically addressing issues of diversity, access, equity, and inclusion. As the national and global landscapes continue to evolve, there is a particular urgency to provide substantial attention to the promotion of change at institutions of higher education. As such, chief diversity officers must ensure their leadership has the innate ability to impact the climate in tangible, measurable ways.

CAMPUS CLIMATE

Campus climate impacts all facets of institutional life and resonates as the most critical issue institutions face. Whether it is working to address student concerns that have been sparked by national issues or agendas, meeting to discuss the experiences of faculty and staff on campus, or responding to concerns expressed by political or community constituents, issues of climate are central to the importance of a chief diversity officer being the primary change agent at an institution.

In the context of higher education, the references to campus climate refer to the culture of an institution in relation to the respect and civility extended to college constituents. Climate involves the attitudes and behavior that are present and exhibited at the college by faculty, staff, and students. Campus climate also involves the efforts by the institution itself to support a welcoming and nurturing environment for all. It must also be noted that the campus climate can be impacted by the external community as well as relevant and timely current events and occurrences in the community, region, nation, or abroad.

WHY DOES CAMPUS CLIMATE MATTER?

The campus climate at an institution is important as it refers to the experiences and treatment of individuals at the institution. It directly examines how various constituents experience the institution and how they are treated. Climate is critical to the sustainability of a college or university because how an individual is treated and what they experience directly impacts their academic outcomes, retention, hiring, and perception of the organization.

An important first step of being a change agent in addressing issues of climate as a chief diversity officer is the ability to ensure the frequent examination of the pulse of the climate on campus. Whether it is an internal climate study to gauge student, faculty, and staff experiences in terms of feeling properly supported or collaborative efforts with various campus constituencies to monitor morale, respect, and civility, the necessity for the frequent execution of the review of the campus climate is of paramount importance to the role of the chief diversity officer.

The frequent monitoring of the campus experience and a general "temperature check" at the institution provides vital information to change agents on the most pressing issues at the institution and allows the chief diversity officer to understand what items need to be on their professional radar. Insight into potential percolating issues and the pressing issues/concerns of the day are primary targets for those working to address effective change.

An appropriate and necessary skill for chief diversity officers is the awareness and understanding of relevant tools to examine climate at institutions. As a primary responsible party to execute the reviews, chief diversity officers must be aware of the appropriate components of a climate study. They must understand how to execute these survey tools and provide guidance to effectively utilize these studies at their respective institutions. Whether it is working directly with a consulting group or with internal constituents, chief diversity officers must be a part of the institution's leadership team to execute institutional campus climate studies.

Many chief diversity officers have often observed colleges working reactively to address critical issues that have emerged "out of nowhere" and become a crisis or major cause of concern. While these instances will undoubtedly occur, more often than not these issues were already very present, swirling in conversation circles and readily available for discussion at campuses. Chief diversity officers who are diligent in their review of campus climate enter their positions armed with extensive knowledge of the issues facing their particular organizations and have a broader understanding of the working and learning environment of the institution.

Utilizing campus climate studies for a continuous and timely review of the sentiments and perceptions of students, faculty, and staff are pertinent tools in avoiding an institutional climate that is "reactive" to issues, incidents, and concerns. A reactive culture of response refers to an institution and leadership group that is limited in terms of being informed and aware of the culture and experiences of its constituents. Simply put, reactive culture refers to an environment in which a campus leadership group is not aware or waits for an issue or concern to arise to respond.

Proactive campus climate response refers to an environment in which the culture and experiences of campus constituents are frequently assessed and reviewed to prioritize responses. This involves intentional outreach and check-ins with faculty, staff, and students to gauge their experiences at the institution. Colleges that are proactive campus climate response institutions utilize a number of tools, including campus climate studies, open dialogue sessions, online forums to provide review, and various participation organizations to facilitate feedback from campus constituents. These institutions are the most aware and informed as incidents concerning climate and experience emerge at the institution.

It is this work that is critical to a chief diversity officer's ability to serve as the primary change agent of campus climate and the individual who can respond more expediently to issues that may potentially lead to crisis. Indeed, being a proactive change agent of campus climate can better assist with strategic relationships of need and provide insight into appropriate next steps to help support institutions of higher education in promoting diversity, equity, and inclusion as institutional priorities.

FACULTY REPRESENTATION AND BUY-IN

Diverse representation in faculty is an essential component of institutions that prioritize inclusion, equity, and access for all. Diversity in faculty representation ensures not only a variety of demographic backgrounds of those providing instruction at the institution but also diversity in thought, ideology, and curriculum development. Higher education faculty are on the front line of engaging and executing the mission of the college or university; therefore, it is essential for organizations to be committed to attracting and retaining faculty who represent diverse backgrounds. That diversity must include thought and perspective as well as differences in race, class, gender, sexual orientation, ability, and so forth.

It is essential that chief diversity officers be not only on the front line but also in the trenches, working to attract and retain a diverse faculty at their respective institutions. A chief diversity officer working as the primary change agent must be in the forefront, advocating for the priority of the attraction of diverse talent. Given the challenges in the pipeline of diverse faculty to tenure-track faculty positions, change agent chief diversity officers must work to create programs that bring attention to the need for greater diversity in faculty ranks.

For certain institutions, this might be a faculty fellow program; for others, it might be a retention effort or an affinity group. No matter the tool, an intentional effort must be executed to raise awareness to and bring about the execution of the programs to support diverse representation in the faculty ranks.

In addition to the attraction and retention of faculty, the necessity for creating and facilitating buy-in and collaboration with faculty is essential for chief diversity officers to fulfill their roles as change agent. Chief diversity officers who understand this role understand the necessity for faculty champions to help push forward new initiatives to support inclusion.

Indeed, the buy-in and collaboration with faculty can add increased volume on messages to promote change and can bring additional audiences and resources. Chief diversity officers and all constituents realize that it is nearly impossible to promote new initiatives at a college or university without the buy-in of faculty. It is the necessity of this relationship that makes the priority for collaboration and partnership essential for chief diversity officers that are working as change agents.

ATTRACTION, RETENTION, AND INVOLVEMENT OF A DIVERSE STUDENT BODY

Now more than ever, given the changing population demographics in the United States and shifts toward a global market in postsecondary education, colleges and universities must prioritize the attraction of a diverse student body. An expanding market of competition catapults the need for colleges and universities to be intentional in providing accessibility for all and promoting a welcoming environment for students from varying backgrounds and experiences.

The diverse representation for students may include race, gender, sexual orientation, political affiliation, gender identity and expression, cognitive and physical ability, and veteran status, as well as any other descriptors and qualifiers in diversity. It is these demographic categorization representations that promote an educational experience in which difference is present in not only the makeup of people but also the academic class in environment and the experiences had on the campuses both inside and outside the classroom. The presence of this difference is essential to preparation for the contemporary global society.

For chief diversity officers working as change agents in their service to colleges and universities, they must be intentional in effort to ensure that diverse recruitment for student populations is a priority. An expanded presence of various demographic populations is at the very center of change to an institution. Chief diversity officers must be involved in the process to attract and retain diverse student populations. They must be at the table when discussing the execution of the strategies of recruitment.

In order to galvanize greater support for the attraction of diverse student populations, a close relationship with enrollment management staff is a necessary component to identify plans of action to attract diverse students. An investment like this requires periodic review of the recruitment processes and operations of the division, appropriate diversity and cultural sensitivity training, and review of program operations including, but not limited to, diverse preview/visitation days.

Effort must be made to ensure a welcoming climate for new students along with a review of material used for recruitment to observe the visual representation of diverse student, faculty, and staff. Additionally, the chief diversity officer must require that institutions be intentional in reaching out to populations that might be traditionally marginalized. It is this effort that is an essential step in attracting students who may have traditionally been overlooked by the institution and works to promote change in the demographic makeup of the institution.

Chief diversity officers working as change agents must also be attentive to the retention of students of diverse backgrounds. In this role, they must use appropriate information and data to examine appropriate resources, including scholarship and support services, that are necessary to assist student populations with the maturation and advancement in the educational experience.

An expansion of the population of diverse and traditionally underrepresented student populations may require additional support services at the institution. These services are essential not only for the attraction of students but also to assist with retention support. It is the role of the chief diversity officer to push the institution to examine equity and access of support services for all populations while promoting positive outcomes for marginalized populations. Simply put, the push toward inclusion goes beyond attraction. The investment in students and student success must be sustained throughout the educational experience.

It is the responsibility of the chief diversity officer to partner with faculty and other administrative colleagues to more deeply examine the academic success of diverse student populations using data and information. Insight and examination of this information should provide guidance on the appropriate support areas and should illuminate the need for resources to assist various populations with being successful. It should be noted that no effort to attract students is fully complete without a complementary effort to retain them. Now more than ever, working to be an agent of change in higher education requires pushing institutions to be more attentive to the importance of completion and academic success of diverse student populations.

Chief diversity officers must work with different institutional stakeholders at the academy to address the issues that have the ability to be shaped. It simply is not enough to attract a diverse student population. Greater work and institutional collaboration must be implemented to retain students of various backgrounds. The chief diversity officer must provide periodic review of supportive services—both academic and social, in terms of student engagement—to examine the priority and level of commitment for retaining and supporting a traditionally underrepresented student population.

When certain student populations are not academically productive and are negatively impacted in retention numbers, the chief diversity officer must intervene and be a change agent to make sure that the appropriate resources are allocated to provide holistic support for the student populations in need. Whether it is the intervention in tutoring and academic support for writing or making an institutional push for additional support for student organizations that primarily serve diverse student populations, the chief diversity officer must be a change agent to make sure that the proper attention is provided to these vehicles as support for students.

DIVERSITY ADVISORY COMMITTEES

An additional tool of resource for chief diversity officers that are agents of change is institutional diversity committees. As chief diversity officers work to enact change, the need for having a body at the institution to provide additional support and guidance is a priority. Whether it is providing information on the happenings at the institution or working to execute recommendations that have been identified as a priority for the institution, diversity advisory committees are a tool of benefit for institutions to enact the recommendation of change to support diversity and equity at the institution.

These support bodies can take any number of names and should involve support and guidance from the institutional president. These committees should be composed of constituents throughout the institutions, including faculty and staff, and must involve participation and oversight from the chief diversity officers. For these bodies, chief diversity officers must set the agenda and provide primary oversight. Chief diversity officers can use these bodies to execute college-wide initiatives to enact change and transformation.

ACCESS TO STUDENT VOICES

Access to student voices is a paramount issue for the chief diversity officer. As was the case with the University of Missouri and other institutions that have faced turmoil with issues of inclusion, diversity, and access, the voice of student concerns emerged as a critical and essential issue to be addressed. Chief diversity officers who are working to be agents of change must work with the appropriate staff, faculty, and student liaisons to have an ongoing understanding of the experiences of students as well as their perceptions of the institution and leadership of the institution.

Chief diversity officers must be intentional and diligent in outreach to students. They must utilize various means to attract students to extract information on their experiences and perceptions of the institution. At times, chief diversity officers might utilize town hall forums and online survey tools in addition to attending various student leadership efforts, including student organizations/student union meetings, to harvest feedback.

The chief diversity officer must advocate for different vehicles to gauge and harvest student experiences and perspectives in relation to their collegiate journey. It is the role of the chief diversity officer to gather this information and share it with key stakeholders, including the senior leadership team and other constituents, to make sure that the voice of students is a priority for the institution.

POLICIES, PROCEDURES, AND COMPLIANCE INITIATIVES

Policies, procedures, and compliance initiatives are essential subjects for the work agenda of the chief diversity officer. These subjects will be examined more in depth in a later chapter; however, it is important to note that the work in these subjects is essential to the role of the chief diversity officer working proactively to be a change agent. Appropriate attention to challenge, address, and change policies and procedures that attend to the needs of diverse populations is essential.

The change agent component of this work is to guide institutions toward adopting new policies and procedures that are proactive and not reactive for creating an inclusive and welcoming environment for all campus constituents. This push toward addressing policy requires open communication from various college/university stakeholders, as well as communication with legal resources and an ongoing review of issues impacting students, faculty, and staff. Chief diversity officers must be informed on policy shifts and changes as it relates to the Department of Education's Office for Civil Rights. A close working relationship with the organization's general counsel is also advised.

While there are specific legal, regulatory, and compliance-related changes that institutions must adhere to, it is the responsibility of the chief diversity officer to promote greater policy shift in access, inclusion, and equity. Whether it is addressing issues on hiring diverse constituents, creating an environment that is inclusive for gender identity and expression, or examining compliance with the Americans with Disabilities Act in facilities, the chief diversity officer must be on the forefront of creating change at the institution and appropriately addressing issues of policy and procedure.

It should be noted that working directly with key stakeholders, including students, faculty, and staff, is essential in gathering information on policies and procedures of interest and in need of review by the president's cabinet and approved by the board of trustees.

Student, faculty, and staff support has been continuously referenced as essential for working as a change agent or as a chief diversity officer. While these constituents are important, so, too, is the facilitation of a relationship with members of the cabinet or senior leadership team while garnering support from the board of trustees. Chief diversity officers must be intentional with setting an agenda that involves the blessing of the president of the college and one that is communicated with the broader cabinet. As the cabinet is the organizational senior leadership team, they will be critical resources in helping to allocate the necessary resources to address issues of inclusion and to work proactively in addressing and promoting change.

It should also be noted that the senior leadership team has the ability to influence managers to execute operations and to enforce the appropriate policies and procedures that work to address issues of diversity, access, and inclusion. A chief diversity officer must be intentional with keeping the lines of communication open with the cabinet and making sure not only to push the agenda but also to listen to the agenda items and initiatives of fellow cabinet members to help promote holistic inclusion at the institution.

While a relationship with the leadership team and cabinet is essential, direct access and partnership with the president of the institution is a priority. Chief diversity officers must have a direct line to the college president to garner support and to inform the president of relevant and timely issues impacting the institution. It should be the chief diversity officer who is the primary liaison to the president on matters impacting diversity and inclusion. While it is in most instances the college president's ultimate call to enact institution-wide change, the chief diversity officer should be the primary counsel to advise in matters of inclusion to promote that change.

A deeper level of support for being an agent of change as a chief diversity officer is in the relationship with the board of trustees. Even though not every chief diversity officer has access to the board of trustees directly, it is important to work toward establishing a relationship that can provide access to the board and to gain a deeper and more robust platform to share ideas and perspectives that promote diversity and inclusion. This essential need to have a relationship with the board of trustees is an expedited way at times to push the initiatives of diversity and inclusion forward.

BEING A STRATEGIC LIAISON TO ALL COLLEGE CONSTITUENTS

A chief diversity officer working to promote change must be a liaison for all college constituents and must understand that at varying times this position must be the sounding board for various ideas and experiences of constituents throughout the campus community. Whether it is a discussion regarding issues of climate and the experiences of students or faculty looking at equity in hiring and expanded opportunities to attract diverse faculty, chief diversity officers need to understand that they must be attending to the college constituents' needs when setting the agenda for diversity, equity, and inclusion.

While the chief diversity officer must ultimately be responsible for the operations that promote diversity and inclusion at the institution, it is an overall institutional commitment with "buy-in" and support from all constituents working proactively that promotes an environment of change.

Chief diversity officers must be ever present and attentive to times, spaces, and places to build strategic relationships with various stakeholders to help promote change. Previously, the chapter discussed the relationship with students, staff, and faculty. Chief diversity officers must meet these constituents where needed to fortify relationships to enact change. Whether it is at employee resource group meetings, faculty governance meetings, student government meetings, or academic department meetings, chief diversity officers must be present and approachable to build rapport and relationships to promote and support change.

Chief diversity officers' constant work to cultivate relationships and harvest perceptions are essential to positively impact change as it relates to diversity, equity, and the promotion of inclusive excellence agendas.

LEVERAGE INSTITUTIONAL/COMMUNITY RESOURCES WHEN NEEDED

At various times when working to address issues of change and serving as a change agent, there may be a need for broader community support and information for specific issues. Chief diversity officers must be open to fostering relationships with various community and political constituents to have a positive and productive platform to address issues of policy and to have better access to resources to advance diversity agendas.

Depending on the jurisdiction, there may be greater resources in the external community to help assist with promoting change to move the institution forward. Chief diversity officers must understand that it is the greater community that makes up and directly impacts the institutional community. It is the chief diversity officer's role to serve and bring together all constituents and, more important, to listen to broader agendas to work to address the institution.

DIVERSITY STRATEGIC PLANS

In their effort to work as change agents, chief diversity officers must promote an institutional culture that is fluid and proactive in addressing issues of diversity, equity, and inclusion. In pursuit of this work, chief diversity officers must have a guide, map, or lynchpin to direct their work. As a means of executing change, chief diversity officers must be the architects and the ultimate responsible party for a strategic plan to impact inclusion to push forward their work as change agents to impact equity, diversity, and inclusion.

As chief diversity officers work to establish strategic plans at their respective institutions, they must ensure that these plans are within direct correlation and collaboration with the overall institutional strategic plan. In fact, before commencing work on a diversity strategic plan, it is advised that chief diversity officers work in collaboration with institutional research and college planning to influence and impact the broader college-wide strategic plan.

Executing this work ensures that issues of inclusion are brought to the forefront for the college-wide strategic plan and further expanded upon in the execution of the diversity strategic plan. In executing this partnership, diversity and inclusion work becomes a priority for the institution at the highest levels. The foundational work in the broader strategic plan is now the lynchpin for a diversity "plan of action" that will take the form of the diversity strategic plan.

FOUNDATIONS FOR STARTING

A foundation must be laid for the chief diversity officer to work to enact actionable change in the form of an invested strategic plan. The origin for this effort begins at the college through the relationships that will be used to harvest committee participation and support of this work. The chief diversity officer must work with various constituents to gather relevant institutional perspectives (cultural climate perceptions), information on pressing concerns, and work with leadership, including the college's president, to identify the aspirational goals. This work is essential in moving forward with an effort to construct a diversity strategic plan.

Pushing this work forward involves a strategic review of where the institution currently stands in terms of relevant data that impacts inclusion including the recruitment, retention, and completion of students. It should include the previously noted cultural climate study data, the demographic makeup of the institution, data and information on hiring and retention of diverse faculty and staff, relevant information on policy, and the institution's adherence to relevant compliance mandates. Lastly, this review should include the assessment of community partnerships, engagement with the K–12 pipeline and other postsecondary institutions, and partnership and procurement expenditures with minority, women, and disadvantaged-owned businesses.

Once the appropriate assessment has been executed, the chief diversity officer should work to coordinate a college-wide committee to serve as the drafting party or the executing committee to compile and complete the diversity strategic plan. This committee should be intentionally inclusive in terms of diverse representation and should reach across the institution to include members of the faculty, administration, and staff. The chief diversity officer should be responsible for the review of the makeup of the committee to ensure diverse perspectives and experiences. Where appropriate, the chief diversity officer should work to identify additional parties to serve in constructing the diversity tactical plan.

As critical issues such as hiring and recruitment will be included and addressed in the diversity strategic plan, it is advised that members of the admissions/recruitment staff be included in the planning team along with members of human resources. These parties will help add perspective and support to potentially identified recruitment efforts of faculty, staff, and students.

The academic agenda for the institution is a priority. Whether it is the discussion of curriculum changes, expansion of majors/programs, expansion of course offerings, or academic assessment, including relevant diversity and inclusion efforts tied to the academic mission of the institution is a priority for any diversity strategic plan. Indeed, it is imperative for any institution promoting inclusion in a strategic plan to appropriately examine the academic outreach of the institution. As such, academic deans, department chairs, and other faculty are essential in both constructing and executing the diversity strategic plan. Simply put, these parties must be directly involved in every facet of this process.

Once an appropriate committee has been organized, the group should begin meeting to execute the work of constructing an appropriate plan to benefit the institution. This body should give significant consideration to identify and prioritize at least five institutional goals that are of importance for the college. While these goals should be aspirational, they should also be obtainable based upon the mission, vision, size, and structure of the institution. Appropriate thought should be given to identify and make available the necessary tools and resources to reach these goals.

While the chief diversity officer is the ultimate responsible party for guiding this plan, various constituents and appropriate stakeholders should be identified as responsible trustees to see this plan through. This body must be provided appropriate direction and the necessary and relevant resources to execute this plan. Once the plan has been articulated and the resources have been identified, the work to enact change is underway.

For the benefit of this text, an example from the Community College of Allegheny County (Pittsburgh, Pennsylvania) is included in appendix B. This resource guide lays out a multi-year Diversity Tactical Plan for Inclusion. Note that in addition to the goals articulated in this strategic plan, appropriate actions, identified partners (responsible parties), and measures or time frames are also indicated. These components identify not only what the institution wants to accomplish but also the appropriate action steps, the relevant partners, and the time frame to complete each goal.

Table 7.1. Diversity Tactical Plan Example

Diversity tactical plan example as found in appendix B

Component 2: Diverse Student Engagement and Retention

	Action	Partners	Measure/Timeframe
Action 1	Identify designated space on campuses for dialogue, resource materials, and diversity programming	CDO, campus presidents and student life department	• Identify temporary space • Identify permanent space by 2014
Action 2	Identify resources and space for interfaith initiatives	Campus presidents, faculty, and staff	• Identify dedicated space for interfaith initiatives by 2014
Action 3	Increase and support the number of diverse student affinity groups to promote student involvement	CDOs, student life department, faculty, staff, and community partnerships	• Ongoing
Action 4	Develop course for diversity educational module for implementation into SDS 102 curricula system-wide	Student support specialist, counselors, and faculty chair for developmental studies	• Develop and incorporate Train the Trainer facilitation module for all SDS 102 instructors by spring 2013
Action 5	Develop additional support services and resources for ESL and international students	Community-based organizations, faculty, and Allegheny campus admissions department	• Expansion of ESL course offering college-wide • Develop college-wide peer-mentoring program for international (F-1) students
Action 6	Identify additional funding streams	Foundation	• Ongoing

As institutions work proactively to address the areas of priority for their inclusion goals, they must identify the appropriate steps to reach their goals, as well as the resources necessary to meet their outcomes. While it is the work of the chief diversity officer to be a change agent at the institution, it is ultimately a college-wide commitment to make this push a reality.

As is articulated in the example provided in appendix B, institutions must be proactive in identifying the relevant goals of priority that meet their aspirations. Upon identifying these goals, they must put in place the appropriate resources and responsible partnerships to achieve their aspired outcomes. It is ultimately the work of the chief diversity officer working as a change agent to make sure that this agenda is advanced. The chief diversity officer must be diligent in oversight of the diversity strategic plan and make sure that responsible parties are observing the appropriate effort to meet the goals.

In situations in which there might be a delay in advancing the goals or hesitancy with addressing the identified priority areas, the chief diversity officer must leverage their power and relationships with the president and cabinet to move the plans forward. The CDO must make the concerns plain.

The chief diversity officer must continuously leverage relationships to galvanize college-wide support and understanding of the shared responsibility for the strategic plan. In instances when advancing the inclusive excellence agenda might stall or meet some opposition, it is up to the chief diversity officer to use this plan to push the college forward to address inclusion and ultimately be the champion of change at the institution.

As chief diversity officers push their work forward as a catalyst for change, they must be intentional in utilizing diversity strategic plans. They must understand that relationships are essential to their work in enacting change. They must garner both the support and the perspectives of faculty, staff, and students to be agents of change. They also must connect with appropriate leadership and leadership bodies to make inclusion a priority at the institution. It is this work that is necessary and timely in making sure that they truly are a catalyst for change.

Archetypes of the Various Chief Diversity Officer Structures and Models

By now you should be familiar with the various structures, models, roles, and responsibilities of chief diversity officers in higher education. The purpose of this chapter is to provide examples of the various archetypes (that is, personalities and characteristics) of a chief diversity officer. It includes a questionnaire that will help senior-level officials and aspiring chief diversity officers understand the particular nuances, challenges, and perspectives of these senior-level positions within the field of higher education.

CDO TYPE INDICATOR QUESTIONNAIRE

The Chief Diversity Officer Type Indicator Questionnaire was developed to provide senior-level officials, as well as current and aspiring chief diversity officers, an opportunity to develop an appreciation for the various structures, roles, and environments in which chief diversity officers operate within the field of higher education. Matching talent and temperament with structures and priorities will inform both institutions and individuals of the particular skills, credentials, and experiences needed in order to successfully achieve the goals of the institution.

The questionnaire is not intended to be an exact science or a perfect assessment. Instead, it was developed to provide institutional leaders and diversity professionals with a better understanding of the ideal conditions, as well as the preferred skills, characteristics, and environments, that best suit the needs of the institution and the position.

Directions

Below is a list of sixteen questions. For each question, please circle the answer that best describes how you or others currently perform or envision the work of the chief diversity officer within the field of higher education.

1. Presentations on diversity, equity, and inclusion are:
   a. cross-divisional and conducted by various departments and constituency groups.
   b. shared by the CDO and a number of dedicated faculty and staff.
   c. the sole responsibility of the CDO, office, department, or division for diversity.
2. Strategic initiatives for diversity are:
   a. determined by a system of shared governance.
   b. shared by the CDO and a number of dedicated faculty and staff.
   c. the sole responsibility of the CDO, office, department, or division for diversity.
3. Addressing incidents of discrimination and bias on my campus is:
   a. cross-divisional and conducted by various departments and constituency groups.
   b. shared by the CDO and a number of dedicated faculty and staff.
   c. the sole responsibility of the CDO, office, department, or division for diversity.
4. Advancing the institution's vision and mission for diversity is:
   a. cross-divisional and conducted by various departments and constituency groups.
   b. shared by the CDO and a number of dedicated faculty and staff.
   c. the sole responsibility of the CDO, office, department, or division for diversity.
5. The infusion of diversity in the curriculum is:
   a. cross-divisional and conducted by various departments and constituency groups.
   b. shared by the CDO and a number of dedicated faculty and staff.
   c. the sole responsibility of the CDO, office, department, or division for diversity.

6. Addressing student outcomes for diversity, equity, and inclusion is:
   a. cross-divisional and conducted by various departments and constituency groups.
   b. shared by the CDO and a number of dedicated faculty and staff.
   c. the sole responsibility of the CDO, office, department or division for diversity.
7. Information related to issues of nondiscrimination, access, and equity in higher education institutions is:
   a. cross-divisional and conducted by various departments and constituency groups.
   b. shared by the CDO and a number of dedicated faculty and staff.
   c. the sole responsibility of the CDO, office, department, or division for diversity.
8. Responsibility for the ongoing engagement and development of institutional policies and procedures on diversity is:
   a. cross-divisional and conducted by various departments and constituency groups.
   b. shared by the CDO a number of dedicated faculty and staff.
   c. the sole responsibility of the CDO, office, department, or division for diversity.
9. Institutional programs, trainings, and workshops on diversity are:
   a. cross-divisional and conducted by various departments and constituency groups.
   b. shared by the CDO and a number of dedicated faculty and staff.
   c. the sole responsibility of the CDO, office, department, or division for diversity.
10. Institutional inquiry, data, and assessment on diversity, equity, and inclusion are:
    a. cross-divisional and conducted by various departments and constituency groups.
    b. shared by me as well as a number of dedicated faculty and staff.
    c. the sole responsibility of the CDO, office, department, or division for diversity.

11. The development and update of metrics, protocols, and controls to mea-
    sure issues of institutional compliance is:
    a. cross-divisional and conducted by various departments and constitu-
       ency groups.
    b. shared by the CDO and a number of dedicated faculty and staff.
    c. the sole responsibility of the CDO, office, department, or division for
       diversity.

12. Communication on institutional diversity efforts at the community, re-
    gional, and national level is primarily:
    a. cross-divisional and conducted by various departments and constitu-
       ency groups.
    b. shared by the CDO and a number of dedicated faculty and staff.
    c. the sole responsibility of the CDO, office, department, or division for
       diversity.

13. The oversight and coordination for advisory boards and committees on
    diversity are:
    a. cross-divisional and conducted by various departments and constitu-
       ency groups.
    b. shared by the CDO and a number of dedicated faculty and staff.
    c. the sole responsibility of the CDO, office, department, or division for
       diversity.

14. Responsibility for addressing the potential barriers that faculty face in
    the promotion and/or tenure process in the context of diversity-related
    professional activities (for example, teaching, research, service) is:
    a. cross-divisional and conducted by various departments and constitu-
       ency groups.
    b. shared by the CDO and a number of dedicated faculty and staff.
    c. the sole responsibility of the CDO, office, department, or division for
       diversity.

15. The ongoing training, consultation, and technical assistance on diversity,
    EEO/discrimination, institutional equity, VAWA, Clery, and Title IX for
    all members of the campus community, with specialized training content
    for hearing officers/boards, investigators, campus law enforcement, and
    appeals officers are:
    a. cross-divisional and conducted by various departments and constitu-
       ency groups.

b. shared by the CDO and a number of dedicated faculty and staff.

c. the sole responsibility of the CDO, office, department, or division for diversity.

16. The responsibility and application of campus climate research in the development and advancement of a positive and inclusive campus climate for diversity is:

a. cross-divisional and conducted by various departments and constituency groups.

b. shared by the CDO and a number of dedicated faculty and staff.

c. the sole responsibility of the CDO, office, department, or division for diversity.

Table 8.1. CDO Type Indicator Scoring Sheet

	I				II				III				IV		
	A	B	C		A	B	C		A	B	C		A	B	C
1				2				3				4			
5				6				7				8			
9				10				11				12			
13				14				15				16			

Scoring

To identify your ideal chief diversity officer position/archetype, use the CDO Type Indicator Scoring Sheet (table 8.1):

1. Place an "x" in the a, b, or c column for each of the sixteen questions.
2. Next, add up the number of a, b, or c answers for each column (each column has a total of four questions).
3. Determining your preferred archetype: whichever of the columns marked I, II, III, or IV have the most "x"s represents your preferred archetype:

I = Community Outreach Officer

II = Employee Officer

III = Compliance Officer

IV = Change Agent

4. Determining your preferred vertical model structure: whichever of the columns marked "A" "B" or "C" have the most "x"s represents your preferred vertical structure model:

A = Collaborative Model
B = Unit-Based Model
C = Portfolio Divisional Model

5. Locate your preferred CDO archetype using table 8.2.

Table 8.2. Chief Diversity Officer Indicator Archetype Matrix

Collaborative community outreach *The Engager*	Unit-based community outreach *The Partner*	Portfolio divisional community outreach *The Stakeholder*
Collaborative employee *The Diplomat*	Unit-based employee *The Advocate*	Portfolio divisional employee *The Delegate*
Collaborative compliance *The Intermediary*	Unit-based compliance *The Enforcer*	Portfolio divisional compliance *The Authoritarian*
Collaborative change agent *The Visionary*	Unit-based change agent *The Implementer*	Portfolio divisional change agent *The Activist*

6. Now take a moment to review the description for your preferred CDO archetype.

THE COLLABORATIVE OFFICERS

Collaborative Community Outreach: *The Engager*

Engagers are adept at developing and fostering relationships between a variety of stakeholders (faculty, staff, students, local business and community leaders, etc.). They are able to make connections between institutional and community initiatives. They are also able to entrench themselves in particular segments or populations of the community that historically have been untapped. They may be sought after to make presentations about their role and, in particular, the challenges of doing the work as the "the only one."

Engagers seek opportunities. Given that they have limited resources, they are constantly devising creative ways not only to capitalize on but also to seize opportunities from a number of internal and external sources. This may not always bode well with other campus officials who are focused on current college priorities and strategic goals. In fact, engagers will routinely find themselves at odds with senior-level and campus officials who are often concerned with creating "initiative fatigue" for various members of the institution.

Collaborative Employee: *The Diplomat*

Diplomats are just that. They are an appointed official of the college or university who must positively interact with and represent the needs and interests of a diverse constituency of stakeholders, both internally and externally. They may hold regular meetings or focus group discussions with underrepresented faculty, staff, and students. And they may report their particular needs and interests with senior-level officials as well as other groups across the college or university.

Although their power is often symbolic in nature, diplomats are able to yield high levels of influence and privilege as they can leverage their collaborative positions of authority to implement institutional change. Conversely, one of the challenges of being a diplomat is that sometimes it can be difficult for stakeholders to trust them. That is, because they represent the needs and interest of every group, some groups may question whether the diplomat has their best interest in mind. Therefore, diplomats must constantly work to engender stakeholder trust.

Collaborative Compliance: *The Intermediary*

Intermediaries are often thought of as the unofficial ombudsperson of the institution. Although they are not responsible for handling compliance investigations, they routinely receive initial reports or complaints of discrimination and harassment that they refer to and consult with federal compliance officials/officers. As a best practice, they may provide general workshops or presentations on various local, federal, and state laws and policies related to the recruitment and retention of faculty, staff, and students, VAWA, and Title IX, as well as bias incident reporting and awareness programs.

Although they do not enforce college or university policies directly, given their interaction with the compliance officials/officers and internal stakeholders on compliance-related matters, they are very familiar with a number of factors that can positively or negatively impact the experiences of stakeholders from underrepresented or marginalized groups. Further, they will occasionally meet with local and state agencies as well as legal counsel to explore the legal and institutional implications of their role.

Collaborative Change Agent: *The Visionary*

Visionaries are highly driven and motivated individuals who possess excellent problem-solving and interpersonal relations skills. They are the consummate motivator and networker. They are also solution-focused and action-oriented and are adept at connecting the dots with regard to institutional programs and initiatives. Visionaries work well under pressure and can generate a high volume of work in relatively short period of time. While some officials rely on subordinates to accomplish the work, visionaries can quickly identify "who" and "what" they need in order to bring diversity efforts to fruition.

One of the challenges of a visionary is the tendency for them to "go rogue." Collaborative visionaries have endless energy and ideas. At times it may be difficult for college officials and stakeholders to keep pace with all of the programs and initiatives that they are attempting to implement, particularly when these types officers must work collaboratively with individuals who do not report to them directly. Senior-level officials will want to consider how to continually motivate and tap into visionaries in order to maintain institutional stability and sustainability over time.

THE UNIT-BASED OFFICERS

Unit-Based Community Outreach: *The Partner*

Partners are purposeful and intentional in forging relationships with various internal and external stakeholders. Unlike engagers, they are hesitant to collaborate with stakeholders unless there is a direct benefit to their work or their unit. Partners are also very practical in that they tend to view outreach efforts as transactional in nature. They are interested in establishing an even exchange of services between their work and the various stakeholders they serve. Partners can be characterized as benevolent autocrats as they run a tight ship, but it is to the benefit of their unit and the institution.

Partners can appear to be aloof at times. However, they are constantly focused on the needs of the unit and its impact on the institution. It has less to do with being uninterested in working with others and more to do with the task at hand. While they may enjoy attending various campus and community events and celebrations, they are mindful that they must meet routine as well as annual goals and objectives. As such, they may assign certain outreach efforts among their subordinates or direct reports so that they can focus on more tactical and strategic aspects of the work.

Unit-Based Employee: *The Advocate*

Advocates work with other members of their unit to ensure that they are addressing the needs and interests of all employees at their institution. Advocates may be charged with providing specific services to underrepresented or marginalized groups of faculty and staff who work for the institution. Either they or a member of the unit are responsible for leading one or more employee resource or social identity–specific support groups on campus. Advocates work to not only report but also address the needs of the various groups on regular basis.

Advocates are intimately aware of the various policies, practices, and procedures and how they impact the employee experience and, in particular, the experiences of underrepresented or marginalized employees. They work extensively with human resources in the recruitment and onboarding process and routinely compile statistical data and analysis reports on the impact of the institution's efforts to diversify its workforce. In some instances, an advocate may have a staff member within the unit devoted to employee diversity such as a diversity recruiter.

Unit-Based Compliance: *The Enforcer*

Enforcers play a critical role in shaping and establishing a culture of compliance at their institution. Unlike intermediaries, enforcers are responsible for addressing issues of discrimination and harassment for all members of the college or university community. They are also instrumental in developing, updating, and maintaining institutional policies and procedures that protect the interests of protected classes and other underrepresented groups of faculty, staff, and students.

Enforcers or members of their unit may serve as the ombudsperson, the federal compliance officer, or the affirmative action officer at their institution. They are less likely to serve in an advocacy role, as they are charged with ensuring that the institution adheres to local, state, and federal guidelines and procedures. In some instances, they may share joint responsibility for compliance with the human resources office. You may occasionally see them at campus events, but most of their time is devoted to reporting and investigating student and employee claims of harassment and discrimination.

Unit-Based Change Agent: *The Implementer*

Implementers are adept at understanding the operational, tactical, and strategic needs of their unit and its role within the larger institution. Whereas

collaborative officer archetypes are constantly generating ideas and supporting the work of others, implementers are concerned with developing and
growing an array of programs and initiatives that sustain the diversity and
inclusion efforts of their unit over time.

Implementers are similar to their collaborative counterparts in that they
find creative ways to embed their work into every facet of the institution.
They are similar to partners in that they are intentional and purposeful in
connecting their work to various internal and external stakeholders. However,
because they are not the "only one," they are able to sponsor, collaborate, and
participate in various programs and initiatives at the local, regional, and national level. Implementers are also able to foster and maintain relationships to
a greater extent than collaborative officers.

THE PORTFOLIO DIVISIONAL OFFICERS

Portfolio Divisional Community Outreach: *The Stakeholder*

Stakeholders are high-profile, credentialed individuals who are seen as institutional and national thought leaders in the field of diversity and inclusion.
Stakeholders are commonly found at larger institutions such as major research
and flagship universities. As such, they have one or more functional offices or
departments that are cross-divisional in nature. This might include functional
activities in services in enrollment, human resources, institutional research,
public relations, development, and student affairs.

Stakeholders are fully vested members of the campus and local community.
Given their portfolio structure, they have a significant amount of budget and
staff. Thus they are able to engage and form meaningful partnerships with a
wide constituency of cultural and social identity groups. Additionally, they
are also able to sponsor a comprehensive number of programs and initiatives
toward diversity and inclusion at the academic, employee, and institutional
levels. Their outreach efforts are both strategic and operational, as well as assessable and measurable.

Portfolio Divisional Employee: *The Delegate*

Delegates are appointed officials who may serve as one or more first-level,
deputy, or divisional diversity officers at their institution. However, they
can exist at the state system or flagship level as well. Typically, delegates are
responsible for a major unit or department as part of the overall diversity di-

vision. Generally speaking, delegates have their own staff and resources that are separate from the other units within the division. In some instances, these roles can be held by tenured faculty as well as experienced administrators.

One of the benefits of being a delegate is they are responsible for a only certain facet of the diversity operation. This allows them to carve a specific niche or specialty area as part of the overall operation. Conversely, one of the challenges is sometimes there can exist a duplication of efforts between delegates and their direct peers with regard to carrying out similar initiatives on behalf of the division, particularly as it relates to resource allocation and development. Thus delegates must be ever mindful to support the shared mission and vision for all units within the division.

Portfolio Divisional Compliance: *The Authoritarian*

Authoritarians are highly experienced and credentialed professionals in the area of compliance. Unlike enforcers, authoritarians are responsible for addressing issues of compliance at the local, state, and federal levels. They can serve as the leading senior diversity officer, and they may be positioned at a campus, flagship, or state-system office. They need very little supervision to perform the functional duties of their position and work closely with the subordinates to ensure consistency and transparency in the regulatory process. In some instances they may outsource services.

Authoritarians have an ethical, moral, and legal responsibility to ensure that the institution remains compliant in all facets of the operation. Typically, they communicate regularly with high-level officials, trustees, legal counsel, as well as key individuals from state and federal agencies. They either lead or share responsibility for affirmative action programs and policies, more so than their collaborative and unit-based counterparts. Further, they may be called to testify and defend the institution from prosecution, and they may refer stakeholders to public and federal resources in an advocate capacity.

Portfolio Divisional Change Agent: *The Activist*

Activists are game changers. They are highly credentialed and political individuals who are tasked with advancing diversity and inclusion at their campus as well as within the field. They also have a huge responsibility and commitment to providing advocacy and support to underrepresented groups through ongoing trainings and workshops.

Activists work to dismantle existing structures and systems of oppression on an institutional and global level. They have significant portfolio of resources and staff to make substantive change across the institution and beyond. They lead with high levels of authority and autonomy and in some instances are able to make major decisions on behalf of the institution. Given their high level of responsibility, these officers are likely to report directly to the senior leader (that is, president, chancellor, chief executive officer, etc.) for either the institution or the university system.

CONCLUSION

The CDO Type Indicator Questionnaire was developed to provide senior-level officials, as well as current and aspiring chief diversity officers, an opportunity to develop an appreciation for the various structures, roles, and environments in which CDOs operate within the field of higher education. It should serve as both a conversation starter and a planning resource in developing similar roles and functions at your institution. It should also help senior-level officials consider the level of interaction and support that will be needed in order for these positions to be successful.

There is no perfect archetype or condition in which a chief diversity officer operates. As previously stated, the chief diversity officer at institutions of higher education wears many hats of responsibility and fulfills a number of roles in the scope of duties at the organization. Although one may have a preferred archetype, this does not preclude one from taking on the characteristics of another archetype. Thus there are times when the roles and functions of a chief diversity officer are situational.

Take the questionnaire, for example. You probably noticed that in scoring your questionnaire there are times that you or your institution operate under a collaborative model, while other times you might act under a unit-based or portfolio divisional model. Similarly, you may have found at times that you act as a community outreach officer, while at other times you might act as an employee, compliance, or change agent. Once again, one size does not fit all.

As the role of the chief diversity officer continues to evolve, so, too, will the advancement of the various structures and models at college and university campuses. Community colleges in particular will want to consider which of the various CDO indicator types will work best for their community. Given the relatively few positions that currently exist, it will be important to determine which structures and models work best for their internal and external community.

Conclusion

The push toward a global economy and a more inclusive society has brought greater attention to the pressing need to prioritize diversity, equity, and inclusion agendas for organizations. Community colleges, like other organizations and institutions of higher education, must be prepared to engage dialogue and make strategic decisions on the directions and commitment to support diversity, inclusion, and equity. These institutions must have central leadership to help guide, shape, and push forward the work to support an inclusive excellence agenda. Now more than ever, the role of the chief diversity officer is of paramount importance in solidifying institutional leadership to support diversity. These leaders are the intuition's architects in providing strategic direction, guiding policy, and negotiating change.

Chief diversity officers serve as the primary responsible parties for guiding institutional direction toward inclusive excellence, while serving as the primary point of contact for other senior leaders, boards of trustees, faculty, staff, and students. These individuals prioritize for the institution the important areas of compliance management and the need for additional education and competency training around inclusion and create and foster relationships with broad community constituents. Additionally, they work directly to shape curriculum and instruction adjustment to help promote a broader completion agenda for diverse constituents. Simply put, chief diversity officers are critical to the operations of a contemporary twenty-first-century community college.

Given all CDOs do to guide institutional direction, there are still gaps in broad representation of these positions at institutions. A number of community colleges have yet to fully adopt the chief diversity officer model as a senior leadership position at their institutions. In some instances, their work is completed by multiple constituents who work to operationalize, address, and complete the institution's efforts around inclusion. While it is positive for the work to be completed in either instance, gaps exist when units work without the direction of a primary officer to help establish an institutional direction for the inclusive excellence agenda. The institutions may be subject to institutional oversights and possible gaps in the areas of compliance oversight, which can possibly escalate concerns regarding liability and risk.

This text has articulated the various expectations of responsibility for chief diversity officers. Whether the chief diversity officer is working in the capacity of an outreach and engagement officer, serving as an employee officer, managing institutional guidance as a compliance officer, or working as a change agent at the institution, the position responsibilities assert the need for a broad knowledge base and the necessity for guidance and direction.

Professional development support and guidance from organizations like the National Association of Diversity Officers in Higher Education (NADOHE) are an imperative for individuals in these roles. Resources like the NADOHE Standards of Professional Practice for Chief Diversity Officers provide CDOs with a scholarly litmus test from which to measure their work. These tools help prioritize institutional agenda and further guidance on the starting places for chief diversity officers to execute their work.

Critical to discussions regarding diversity and inclusion at institutions of higher education is the conversation around institutional climate and culture. As population demographics shift, the climate and culture of an institution evolve. The constituents who make up an institution and their beliefs and perspectives shape the interactions and exchange. These exchanges have an impact on curriculum and instruction, collegial interactions, and influence the need for appropriate response to climate, policy, and compliance oversight. Chief diversity officers in their various roles negotiate these responses. They are the primary responsible parties at institutions to negotiate change in culture and work to provide overall guidance with these matters.

The expanding population demographic changes in society further underscore the need for broad efforts to expand the attraction of diverse talent. Just as institutions intentionally push for diversity representation in the make-up of student populations, there must be an equal push for diverse representation in the talent population of the human capital of the workforce. Institutions must prioritize broader faculty and staff diversity representation as a targeted effort to mirror the population of the communities for which they serve.

The potential benefits of these efforts include a more welcoming and inclusive workforce, expanded opportunities for creativity given the different perspectives of individuals, and the increased opportunity for cross-cultural dialogue. Chief diversity officers are critical in institutional efforts to promote, attract, and retain diverse talent. CDOs help oversee equity in hiring initiatives and further guide policy to attract and retain diverse talent. Further, chief diversity officers serve as the institutional point of contact to prioritize areas of need for talent recruitment of diverse populations. The required management insight and understanding of policy and compliance guidance elevate these positions in terms of expectation, priority, skill, and competency. Established and seasoned chief diversity officers have the appropriate skill, training, and network to serve at the highest levels of leadership at community colleges, including future CEO positions.

BROADER IMPLICATIONS

As has been articulated in the business case model for diversity, prioritizing inclusion provides significant impact to the organization's bottom line and profit and more broadly expands creativity for positive outcomes. A proper investment in leadership around diversity and inclusion or a chief diversity officer can have significant impact on the bottom line of the institution. Even greater is the expansion of creativity and the broad support constituent representation that impacts favorable institutional climate and educational outcomes. A proper chief diversity officer to provide oversight makes the institution a better place for all.

Community colleges are essential to the contemporary landscape of American higher education. These institutions provide broad open access to education and job training for the largest base of constituents in higher education. They have the most diverse population of students and serve as a gateway for postsecondary education for the masses. Individuals who work for community colleges, including chief diversity officers, have a direct benefit in providing access to higher education to their individual communities. These institutions are located in communities and serve as community partners for programming as well as education.

Community colleges have a significant economic impact on the regions in which they are located. More often than not, community college students who graduate and transfer to four-year institutions, as well as the students who complete job and skill training certificates, live, work, and remain in the region where the institutions in which they study are located. These graduates arm regions with a more educated and skilled workforce. This in turn expands not only the education and skill level of the region's population but also the tax base. Simply put, an investment in the community college is an investment in the job sustainability and economic output of a region.

For chief diversity officers who serve community colleges, they have a direct impact in improving access to these institutions. Additionally, their work in the space of curriculum and policy development can help further expand the representation of diverse individuals who complete their educational pursuits at these institutions.

ASPIRING CHIEF DIVERSITY OFFICERS

For individuals who aspire to be chief diversity officers in the community college setting, there is a host of things that they should work proactively to learn to be better prepared for the role. There are various skills and competencies that need to be appropriately sharpened and learned to prepare for the opportunity. Individuals should learn information about the leadership structure of the institution for which they wish to serve. This information includes an understanding of the current format of the senior leadership team, the structure and oversight of governance of the board of trustees of the organization, information on faculty governance and faculty leadership at the institution, information on the student government, and representation of student leadership at the institution.

Aspiring chief diversity officers must also work proactively to develop the skill of cultivating relationships at the institution. They must form strong working relationships with other colleagues who are part of the senior leadership team and develop relationships with faculty who can provide broad support for the expansion of diversity and inclusion initiatives including curriculum and pedagogy adjustments. They must be diligent in working to cultivate relationships with external community groups who provide support and offer partnership in the space of diversity, equity, and inclusion. They must also develop a direct working relationship with other chief diversity officers who can provide information and resources and offer guidance in working in the diversity space. These relationships are essentials at some point; all chief diversity officers require information, guidance, and support from colleagues.

Individuals who aspire to serve as community college chief diversity officers must have a working knowledge of the expectations of, job skills, and competency areas required for the position. It is advised that they review the chief diversity officer institutional roles articulated in this text. Additionally, they should have a sound working knowledge of the NADOHE Standards of Professional Practice for Chief Diversity Officers in Higher Education.

These aspiring chief diversity officers should connect directly with national organizations including the National Association of Diversity Officers in Higher Education (NADOHE), the American Association of Community Colleges (AACC), and the National Association for Multicultural Education. They should seek to attend national conferences like the annual NADOHE Conference, the National Conference on Race and Ethnicity in American Higher Education (NCORE), the AACC Annual Convention, and various other national, regional, and local conferences.

Similarly, there are expectations for individuals who wish to make the transition from four-year institutions to the community college space in serving as a chief diversity officer. These individuals should work to meet the expectations articulated previously for aspiring chief diversity officers but must also work to familiarize themselves better with the landscape of community colleges. They should work to gain a better understanding of the various programs of study available in the community college.

Chief diversity officers must understand broadly the differences in leadership structure and in terms of working to address the needs of the student constituents and working as a liaison for the broader community. In many instances, the chief diversity officer in community colleges serves as a liaison for a community—based both inside and outside of the institution. As such, it is necessary for these individuals to spend a great deal of time connecting with community organizations and establishing community partnerships to assist with their transition to these positions.

Providing support and guidance to institutional employees is an additional role of responsibility and expectation for chief diversity officers. These individuals provide professional development training and support for the college around the subjects of diversity, equity, and inclusion. They serve as the primary content area experts in guiding training and education in these subjects for institutions. In addition to these roles, CDOs provide conflict resolution support for the institution and facilitate mediations as needed.

COMMUNITY ENGAGEMENT

Chief diversity officers assist with the daily operations of their respective institutions. Those who operate in the role of the chief diversity officer and those who aspire to serve in these positions must work diligently to expand relationships both internally and externally. These professionals must be intentional in developing relationships with multiple constituents both inside and outside of the organization. They must expand competency, skill, and understanding to address inclusive excellence in the community college setting.

For chief diversity officers serving community colleges, there exists a potentially expansive network of support as there are a number of individuals both inside and outside of their organization working to champion equity. Access to this network requires intentional outreach and ongoing communication to develop support and build rapport. Chief diversity officers who are invested broadly in community engagement and outreach are rewarded with access to a broad network of support. These professionals can negotiate relationships with other organizations that support diversity and inclusion and provide additional partnership opportunities, as well as insight and connection to the external community. An example of this might be a more defined partnership with the national or local affiliate of a specific organization working to support diversity, equity, and inclusion in the college's respective geographical region.

CDOS AND LEADERSHIP

In the contemporary framework of higher education, diversity, equity, and inclusion are institutional priorities. Support for an inclusive excellence agenda is a necessity for leaders who wish to make their institutions relevant in providing education and job and skill training to an ever diversifying society and an expanded global economy. College CEOs must empower direct senior-level leadership in the space of diversity and inclusion. CEOs must prioritize the role of the chief diversity officer to the highest level of senior leadership. These leaders must provide the appropriate resource support for the chief diversity officers in terms of staffing, budget resources, education/professional training support, programming development, and an open door of access to provide ongoing insight and guidance on matters of climate, compliance, and other related concerns at the institution.

CEOs must trust chief diversity officers to serve as institutional generals in providing management of policy guidance, to influence budget decisions, and to provide relevant support and recommendations in advancing equity at the institution. CEOs must be willing to empower chief diversity officers to guide, shape, and direct the institution's efforts to be a welcoming and open access point of education and employment for all.

The expansion and attention levied on issues of inclusion in higher education has led to the proliferation of power for chief diversity officers at the academy. The individuals in these roles provide policy management, budget oversight, and strategic leadership and mold the overall directions for the institutions they serve. They are on the front lines of service, working to attract and retain diverse staff, faculty, and students. Their guidance around policy is essential in helping institutions stay compliant on federal and state legislation. Their work is critical in shaping the creativity and vision of organizations that push to meet the needs of the educational market of the twenty-first century. Chief diversity officers and their work make colleges better places for students, faculty, staff, and the broader community.

Afterword

Diversity Leadership and Management in Community Colleges

I am pleased to offer some thoughts and observations about this important work on *Inclusive Directions: The Role of the Chief Diversity Officer in Community College Leadership.* The timing of this book is remarkable, as our community colleges continue to serve our national workforce needs as the most diverse sector in American higher education. With broad goals of service and access, the more than 1,100 community colleges throughout the nation serve nearly half of the undergraduates in all of higher education in the United States and are more racially/ethnically diverse than any other sector of higher education in the United States.

The authors are shaping an important conversation that community colleges must have in the near future as managing diversity, equity, and inclusion in the organizational structures of community colleges cannot be delayed given the rapidly shifting demographics of our nation. As four-year institutions faced similar challenges previously, community college organizational structures will have to define the path forward with developing dedicated leadership strategies for diversity, equity, and inclusion issues because these issues demand standards-based, competent professionals to provide organizational leadership and promote accountability for desired outcomes.

Several years ago, I had the privilege of meeting with national officials of the American Association of Community Colleges, where I learned about the impact and potential of the community college sector to meeting our nation's needs for an educated and technically proficient workforce. It was during those meetings that I first learned of early efforts to manage diversity and inclusion issues and develop leadership models that fit the community college sector.

As the president of the National Association of Diversity Officers in Higher Education (NADOHE), I believe that NADOHE is uniquely positioned to support this discussion focused on chief diversity officers in the community college sector with the publication of our Standards of Professional Practice for Chief Diversity Officers (2014). Furthermore, I am pleased to see how those early conversations about diversity leadership in community colleges have blossomed into this seminal work on CDOs in community college leadership structures. NADOHE stands ready to support our colleagues with their efforts. This book will launch this needed national discussion and position our community college colleagues to more effectively manage the tremendous challenge and opportunity for effective diversity leadership and management in the coming decades.

Archie W. Ervin, PhD
Vice President and Chief Diversity Officer
Georgia Institute of Technology
President
National Association of Diversity Officers in Higher Education

Appendix A

Employee Resource Group Guidelines

EMPLOYEE RESOURCE GROUP GUIDELINES

An employee resource group (ERG) is a group of employees from various employment groups who assist the college in creating an environment and culture that is welcoming and supportive of all employees, particularly those individuals who are members of historically underrepresented populations.

Harper College is committed to recruiting and retaining a diverse faculty and staff. ERGs are supported by the Office of Diversity and Inclusion at Harper College as a means of improving the recruitment and retention of employees from underrepresented populations. Organizations in higher education and the private sector have a long history of partnering with ERGs as a way to build community and to improve recruitment and retention of diverse talent. If you are interested in building community and fostering an environment of inclusion at Harper College, we invite you to complete an application for consideration as a recognized ERG.

ESTABLISHING AN EMPLOYEE RESOURCE GROUP (ERG)

1. Complete an Employee Resource Group Application.
2. List at least five (5) interested employees willing to volunteer to join the group.
3. Identify your target group.
4. Prepare a mission statement for your ERG that is shared with the Office of Diversity and Inclusion.
5. Prepare an introductory message on the benefits of becoming a member of the ERG that will be posted on HIP.
6. The first meeting must be acknowledged by the Office of Diversity and Inclusion.
7. At the first meeting:
   a. Establish a general purpose and mission for your group.
   b. Select a chair, vice chair, and secretary for a one (1)-year term (or term to be determined).
   c. Prepare a list of goals for the group.
   d. Prepare the ERG application, which should be submitted to the Office of Diversity and Inclusion **no later than September 15**.

EMPLOYEE RESOURCE GROUP (ERG) OPERATING PRINCIPLES

1. Members must be employed at Harper College.
2. The group must rely on its members to serve as volunteers.
3. Membership in an ERG is entirely voluntary and shall be open to all employee groups.
4. The ERG may not discriminate in membership or participation.
5. Meetings will be conducted at Harper College.
6. The ERG must be a nonprofit educational organization.
7. The ERG shall not collect dues from its members, nor shall the members receive any compensation, except for reimbursement of expenses.
8. The ERG shall have an annual planning meeting to set goals.
9. The ERG shall host at least one (1) activity during each year such as the following:
   a. Host an outside speaker
   b. Host a career workshop
   c. Host a public service opportunity
   d. Arrange high school tutoring
   e. Attend a conference that is advantageous to the members of the group
   f. Establish a community relations program
   g. Organize events to celebrate and showcase the unique contributions of the ERG members or the communities from which they originate
10. The ERG may have an administrator, other than the special assistant to the president for diversity and inclusion, serve as a sponsor.
11. The ERG shall elect a chair, vice chair, and secretary at each annual meeting (or term to be determined).
12. The ERG may share information with the assigned administrator such as minutes of meetings and event updates.
13. At the end of each fiscal year (**no later than May 15**), the ERG must submit the following to the Office of Diversity and Inclusion:
    a. Records of its accounts and transactions
    b. Annual Report: Were goals met? What worked well? What didn't work well?
    c. Events summary for the year

EMPLOYEE RESOURCE GROUP (ERG) ONLINE APPLICATION

Thank you for your interest in creating an employee resource group at Harper College. An employee resource group (ERG) is a group of employees from various employment groups who assist the college in creating an environment and culture that is welcoming and supportive of all employees but particularly those individuals who are members of historically underrepresented populations.

ERGs are supported by the Office of Diversity and Inclusion at Harper College as a means of improving the recruitment and retention of employees from underrepresented populations. Organizations in higher education and the private sector have a long history of partnering with ERGs as a way to build community and to improve recruitment and retention of diverse talent. If you are interested in building community and fostering an environment of inclusion at Harper College, we invite you to complete an application for consideration as a recognized ERG. Harper College is committed to recruiting and retaining a diverse faculty and staff.

As part of the formal employee resource group application process, Harper College requires that you provide the following information relative to your desired employee resource group.

1. Desired name of your group: _____

2. What is your target membership? _____

3. Mission statement for your group: _____

4. Goals and objectives of the group: _____

5. Please provide an introductory message on the benefits of becoming a member of this ERG. This message will be posted on HIP:

   _____

6. If you have already determined a leadership team (chair, vice chair, and secretary) for your ERG, please list the names of each officer.

   _____

7. Please indicate how much funding the ERG will need from Harper College to carry out its activities for FY 2016. _____

_____

8. Provide a summary of the activities you are planning and how they fulfill the mission of the ERG. _____

_____

9. Has this request for funds been submitted to other sources for funding?

_____

10. How will the effectiveness of your activities be evaluated or measured?

_____

EMPLOYEE RESOURCE GROUP YEAR-END REPORT

TO: Chief Diversity Officer

FROM Employee Resource Group: _____

SUBJECT: Year-End Report for _____

_____

This report summarizes the activities for the employee resource group:

_____

Members' names: _____

Primary goals for current year: _____

Projects or events completed: _____

How did these events or projects help the employee resource group reach its goals?

_____

What goals were not met and still need to be completed?

_____

Future activities: _____

Appendix B

Tactical Plan for Diversity and Inclusion

Tactical Plan for Diversity & Inclusion
2013–2018

October 2016

A Planned Tactical Approach to Transformative Inclusion: 2013–2018

CCAC is committed to fostering an environment of Transformative Inclusion. The college's key goal is a framework that incorporates diversity at its core. Transformative Inclusion is a model involving grounding the academic experience of students and faculty in intellectual rigor that presupposes the importance and complexity of diversity and contributes to the development of the sophisticated intercultural skills necessary to work in a diverse society and interconnected world.

Transformative Inclusion is a commitment to fostering a campus environment that not only recognizes the perspectives, skills, experiences and talents—collectively, "abilities"—of every student, staff and faculty member and administrator, but also cultivates and utilizes those abilities to achieve a more robust, invested and creative campus environment.

In short, Transformative Inclusion is a diversity model designed to yield better participatory diversity and inclusion outcomes.

An institution that has embraced Transformative Inclusion possesses the following characteristics:

1. An open and welcoming campus climate. In concrete terms, it means identifying, promoting, acknowledging and respecting the perspectives of all members of the student body, faculty, staff and community, with particular appreciation for the diverse backgrounds that they all bring to the educational experience.

2. A purposeful development and use of organizational and community-based resources to enhance student success and completion. Organizationally, it means fostering an environment conducive to success with the expectation that faculty, staff and administrators will incorporate inclusiveness in teaching, service, support and outreach.

3. A focus on the cultivation of community partnerships that impact diversity and inclusion in the greater community.

In order to promote Transformative Inclusion as the diversity model and mission for the future of CCAC, this tactical plan outlines six strategic goals, along with a series of measurable implementation actions. The goals of this initiative are to accomplish distinction in the following areas:

1. Expand representation and participation of underrepresented populations and economically disadvantaged individuals in the student body

2. Promote faculty and staff awareness of diversity and inclusion

3. Foster continued growth in the presence of faculty and staff of underrepresented backgrounds

4. Develop and cultivate collaborations and partnerships with community based organizations that promote the mission of diversity and inclusion

5. Increase and sustain MWDBE participation

6. Promote and educate standards of inclusion for the equitable treatment of all individuals

INSTITUTIONAL GOALS

GOAL ONE

EXPAND REPRESENTATION AND PARTICIPATION OF UNDERREPRESENTED POPULATIONS AND ECONOMICALLY DISADVANTAGED INDIVIDUALS IN THE STUDENT BODY

In an effort to make CCAC a more inclusive environment, the college has enacted a goal of expanding the participation and increasing the number of students from underrepresented groups—defined as American Indian/Alaskan; Black or African American; Asian/Pacific Islander; Spanish American (Latino/Hispanic); and Multiracial—as well as economically disadvantaged individuals. A minority recruitment plan was developed in December 2008 and a report presented to the CCAC Board of Trustees in June 2009. This plan was revised and presented to the Board of Trustees in June 2013. This is a living document and continues to develop and expand.

While CCAC is an open-admissions institution and does not require college entrance examinations, enrollment of underrepresented populations at the college has increased over the past decade (see chart below). The enrollment was 3,414 of students reporting a traditionally underrepresented race, in fall 2007. It increased to 3,568 in fall 2008. Federal reporting regulations for 2009 introduced new ethnic/racial categories and required re-reporting of all existing students. Many institutions, including CCAC, have noted a lack of participation in re-reporting under the new regulations, dovetailing with a growing number of individuals nationwide declining to respond to racial/ethnic survey questions. These factors led to a nearly 20% increase in the number of CCAC students not reporting any ethnicity for fall 2009. As a result, the minority headcount appears to drop.

However, CCAC's calculated percentage has always reflected minority students as a percentage of all domestic students who reported race. It ignores students in the "unknown" racial/ethnic category and non-resident aliens. Therefore, even though the number of students self-identifying as minority decreased for 2009, the percentage of minority students to all domestic students reporting race increased to 23%.

Component 1: Diverse Student Recruitment

	Action	Partners	Measure/Timeframe
Action 1	Revise, coordinate and execute diversity recruitment plan	Diversity Recruitment Committee	• July 1, 2013
Action 2	Hire college diversity recruitment specialist. See Appendix 3 for detailed job description.	Human Resources (HR), Student Recruiters and North campus Dean of Student Development	• July 1, 2014
Action 3	Expand and promote self-identity selection and tracking methods	Asst. Dean of Academic Mgt., Advisors, Information Technology Services (ITS), and	• Decrease self-identity non-reporters to 15% by July 1, 2014
Action 4	Expand demographic categorization on forms and electronic format to increase the	Asst. Dean of Academic Mgt., Advisors and	• Decrease self-identity non-reporters to 15% by July 1, 2014

	numbers of self-identified percentages	Information Technology Services (ITS)	

Component 2: Diverse Student Engagement and Retention

	Action	Partners	Measure/Timeframe
Action 1	Identify designated space on campuses for dialogue, resource materials & diversity programming	CDO, Campus Presidents and Student Life department	• Identify temporary space • Identify permanent space by 2014
Action 2	Identify resources and space for inter-faith initiatives	Campus Presidents, faculty and staff	• Identify dedicated space for inter-faith initiatives by 2014
Action 3	Increase and support the number of diverse student affinity groups to promote student involvement	CDO's, Student Life, Faculty, Staff and Community partnerships	• Ongoing
Action 4	Develop course for diversity educational module for implementation into SDS 102 curricula system-wide	Student Support Specialist, Counselors and Faculty chair for Developmental Studies	• Develop and incorporate Train the Trainer facilitation module for all SDS 102 instructors by spring 2013
Action 5	Develop additional support services and resources for ESL and international students	Community based organizations, Faculty and Allegheny Campus Admissions department	• Expansion of ESL course offering collegewide • Develop collegewide peer mentoring program for international (F-1) students.
Action 6	Identify additional funding streams	Foundation	• Ongoing

GOAL TWO

PROMOTE FACULTY AND STAFF AWARENESS OF DIVERSITY AND INCLUSION

CCAC's approach to promoting cultural competency is a collaborative and developmental one. To promote an organizational culture of Transformative Inclusion, the college has committed to offering workshops each semester at the CCAC All-College Day orientation, SEIU Professional Development Day, the Summer Faculty Institute, New Faculty Orientation, College Wide Council and a sustained series of professional development programs. Workshops developed by staff in the Office of Institutional Diversity and Inclusion (OIDI) include, but are not limited to, the following:

- Differences Between Affirmative Action and Diversity
- The Blueprint for Transformative Inclusion
- Diversity, Equity & Inclusion: What We All Need to Know
- Let's Talk about Race
- Diversity is You
- Hate Crimes Against the GLBT community
- Recruitment and Retention of ESL Students
- An Introduction to Racial Micro-aggressions
- Culture and Communications
- Generational Diversity
- Diversity Trends and Institutional Impact

Increasingly, professional development opportunities promoting diversity awareness, multicultural competency and global understanding will be offered through webinars, lectures by visiting content experts, DVDs, movies and CCAC website modules.

	Action	Partners	Measure/Timeframe
Action 1	Maintain and expand collegewide diversity training initiatives for staff, faculty and administration	HR, Academic Affairs, Campus Presidents	• Offer at least one formal collegewide diversity training initiative per semester
Action 2	Include a diversity component to all new hire orientations	HR, Academic Affairs and Professional Development	• July 1, 2013
Action 3	Promote operational definition of Transformative Inclusion and Non-discrimination policy via website and college related print materials	HR, Marketing & Communications	• January 1, 2013
Action 5	Coordinate training program for all supervisors to include diversity component	HR	• July 1, 2013
Action 6	Incorporate a diversity workshop attendance component into annual employee evaluation process	HR	• July 1, 2014
Action 7	Expand and support promotion of Business & Industry in college curriculum	Academic Deans, Faculty Department chairs	• Ongoing

GOAL THREE

FOSTER CONTINUED GROWTH IN THE PRESENCE OF FACULTY
AND STAFF OF UNDERREPRESENTED BACKGROUNDS

Faculty diversification contributes directly to educational quality. A diverse faculty means better educational outcomes for all students. To serve current and future student populations, multiple and diverse perspectives are needed at every level of college teaching and governance. The more diverse college and university faculty are, the more likely it is that all students will be exposed to a wider range of scholarly perspectives and to ideas drawn from a variety of life experiences. The emergence within the last 30 years of new bodies of knowledge can be attributed to the diverse backgrounds and interests of faculty of color. By bringing new research questions and fresh perspectives to the academic enterprise, these scholars create intellectual stimulation for students and faculty alike (Turner 2000; *Shattering the Silence* 1997).

To better serve new students and to prepare all students for an increasingly diverse world, it is important that colleges and universities transform not only what they teach but also how they teach. Evidence suggests that exposure in college to a diverse faculty along with diversified curricula and teaching methods produces students who are more complex thinkers, more confident in traversing cultural differences and more likely to seek to remedy inequities after graduation (Hurtado et al. 1999; Smith and Associates 1997). Furthermore, diverse faculty members provide students with diverse role models and help to provide more effective mentoring for students from underrepresented groups.

Diversity and inclusion are imperative to CCAC's mission and strategic plan. While the college continues to seek diversity in its workforce, it has made impressive gains in the area of employing diverse individuals among the ranks of administrators in the past five years.

In 2011–2012, CCAC focused HR efforts on expanding faculty applicant pools to ensure more diverse representation. This was achieved through new and ongoing initiatives:

- Development and implementation of search committee training sessions
- Incorporating diversity-related questions for all applicants at the formal interview stage
- Expanded marketing and outreach efforts for open positions to diversify applicant pools
- Review of applicant pools to ensure representative minority representation
- Consistent review of search committee compositions
- Increased participation in regional minority candidate recruitment events

CCAC will continue to expand its recruitment efforts to ensure diverse applicant pools. Knowing that diverse search committees can bring a greater variety of viewpoints to the hiring process, the college will continue to monitor the composition of its search committees, encouraging diverse committees that are equipped to find the most qualified candidates for the positions to which they apply. These efforts, among others, are expected to attract and retain more diversity hires and depict CCAC as an employer of choice.

Component 1: Continue to develop and implement equitable hiring practices			
	Action	Partners	Measure/Timeframe
Action 1	Revise and standardize search committee training process	HR and Hiring Administrators	Develop search committee evaluation tool by July 1, 2013

Action 2	Establish search process debriefing sessions for periodic assessment	Hiring Administrator, Search Committee members	Develop by July 1, 2013
Action 3	Identify a greater number of diverse candidate pipelines (regional & national)	HR and Marketing & Communications	Increase applicant pools and marketing efforts for open positions
Action 4	Hire additional staff in HR to focus on diversity recruitment. See Appendix 2 for detailed job description	HR	Establish position in 2014

Component 2: Retention and Professional Development of New Hires

	Action	Partners	Measure
Action 1	Incorporate diversity component into institutional succession plan	HR, Academic Affairs and Campus Presidents	July 1, 2014
Action 2	Introduce and expand participation of campus employee resource or affinity groups for staff and faculty	HR, Academic Affairs and Campus Presidents	Introduce/establish Campus Wellness, Young Professionals, and Interfaith Exploration employees resources groups by July 1, 2014

Bibliography

Cohen, Arthur M., and Florence B. Brawer. *The American Community College*. San Francisco, CA: John Wiley and Sons, 2013.

Committing to Equity and Inclusive Excellence: A Campus Guide for Self-Study and Planning. Washington, DC: Association of American Colleges and Universities, 2015.

Innovation Partners International. http://www.innovationpartners.com/.

Jones, Jackie. "Demanding Inclusion: Will Having More Chief Diversity Officers, as Student Protestors Have Asked, Resolve the Tensions behind the Wave of Protests at Campuses around the Nation?" *Diverse Issues in Higher Education* (2016): 4–8.

Kaleidoscope Group: Your Full Service Diversity and Inclusion Partner. http://kgdiversity.com/.

Mott, Mesha, and Andrés T. Tapia. *Network and Affinity Leadership Handbook, 3rd Edition: The Definitive Guide for Forming, Launching and Engaging Employee Resource Groups*. New York: Diversity Best Practice, 2013.

Thomas, Roosevelt R., and Marjorie I. Woodruff. *Building a House for Diversity: A Fable about a Giraffe and an Elephant Offers New Strategies for Today's Workforce*. New York: Thomas and Associates, 1999.

The Standards of Professional Practice for Chief Diversity Officers. National Association of Diversity Officers in Higher Education, 2014.

Williams, Damon A. *Strategic Diversity Leadership: Activating Change and Transformation in Higher Education*. Sterling, VA: Stylus, 2013.

Williams, Damon A., and Katrina C. Wade-Golden. "The Chief Diversity Officer." *CUPA HR Journal* (2007): 38–47.

———. *The Chief Diversity Officer: Strategy, Structure, and Change Management*. Sterling, VA: Stylus, 2013.

West, Cassandra. "Chicago Fellows: Harper College's Faculty Fellows Program Strives to Establish a Diverse Workforce." *Diverse Issues in Higher Education* (2014): 10–11.

Index

About the Authors

Clyde Wilson Pickett, EdD, currently serves as the special assistant to the president for diversity and inclusion (chief diversity officer) at the Community College of Allegheny County (CCAC) in Pittsburgh, Pennsylvania. Pickett was appointed to this position after a national search in October 2012. Prior to his appointment at CCAC, Pickett served as the director of multicultural diversity/director of new student orientation (associate dean) at Ohio Northern University (ONU) in Ada, Ohio. In this capacity, Pickett led the strategic planning process around diversity and inclusion that resulted in the establishment of the ONU Multicultural Center.

In his current role, Pickett provides college-wide leadership and oversight for diversity, equity, and inclusion agendas. He is a member of the president's cabinet and helps to develop institutional priorities, policies, programs, and initiatives to advance the inclusive excellence agenda. Pickett is responsible for the oversight of the strategic operations of the office of institutional diversity and inclusion (OIDI) and is responsible for helping create the CCAC Diversity Tactical Plan.

Recognized as a national leader in diversity in higher education, Pickett is a member of the Board of Directors for the National Association of Diversity Officers in Higher Education (NADOHE), the nation's leading association of diversity professionals in the United States. He is also the founder of two educational consulting firms that specialize in diversity training, strategic planning, program development, and management services.

Pickett completed his bachelor's degree in agricultural economics from the University of Kentucky and his master's of education in adult and higher education leadership with an emphasis in counseling and multicultural issues from Morehead State University. He completed his doctoral degree in language, literacy, and culture at the University of Pittsburgh's School of Education. A resident of Pittsburgh, Pickett is active in the local community, serving on the board of directors for the Hill House Association, Inc., the Society for Contemporary Craft, and the Pittsburgh Urban Magnet Project.

Michelé Smith, MEd, is currently the associate provost/special assistant to the president for diversity and inclusion at William Rainey Harper College in Palatine, Illinois. Prior to serving in this capacity, Smith served as dean of the business and social science division, full-time faculty in the early childhood education department, and coordinator of the Harper College Child Learning Center. In her current role, Smith is responsible for the leadership of college-wide curriculum, shared governance oversight, and the college's diversity and inclusion initiatives. These initiatives include, but are not limited to, serving as ombudsperson for bias incident reporting, developing support for employee resources groups (ERGs), providing leadership for the diverse faculty fellows program aimed at improving employee diversity in the faculty ranks, and collaborating with human resources on the implementation of 360-degree feedback surveys and web-based exit interviews.

Smith is known as an inspirational leader, practitioner, and scholar who has been dedicated to issues of inclusion and equity for more than twenty years in the academy, the private sector, and the early childhood education community. In 2015, Smith began serving as the executive lead for the Harper College Promise Scholarship Program, which was designed to help every student attending one of the public high schools in the Harper College district earn two years of college tuition free. She has facilitated a number of interactive workshops and education sessions focused on issues of inclusion and multicultural education, served as resource specialist for parents and professionals of young children with special needs, and led a number of summer bridge programs for student scholars from historically underrepresented populations.

Smith is passionate about education and empowerment and firmly believes in the value and transformative impact of diversity and inclusion on the health and sustainability of an institution or organization. She holds a bachelor's degree in psychology from Northwestern University, a master's degree in early childhood education leadership and advocacy from National Louis University, and is currently a candidate for her PhD in educational psychology from Northern Illinois University. Smith is an active member of a number of organizations committed to advancing diversity and inclusion and social justice efforts in higher education.

James A. Felton III, MS, is the inaugural chief diversity officer at SUNY Cortland. Previously he served three years as the inaugural chief diversity officer at Anne Arundel Community College after serving as the inaugural director of intercultural affairs at Western Carolina University in Cullowhee, North Carolina. A noted leader, educator, mentor, and scholar-practitioner in the field of diversity in higher education, Felton has contributed to the development of several diversity and strategic plans including the renowned University of Wisconsin's Plan 2008 (Green Bay campus). He was also responsible for managing three major scholarship and mentor programs for underrepresented students at a number of selective private liberal arts colleges and state-system universities across the country. He has also partnered with corporate, nonprofit, and federal agencies and NGOs to promote international programs and initiatives on diversity and social justice. Most recently, he was appointed the project team leader on behalf of Anne Arundel Community College's participation in the Committing to Equity and Inclusive Excellence initiative sponsored by the Association of American Colleges and Universities (AAC&U).

Felton is a founding member of the Pennsylvania Association of Liaisons and Officers for Multicultural Affairs (PALOMA), a state-wide organization that provides advocacy, support, best practices, and continual renewal for diversity professionals in the field. He also holds memberships with the National Association of Diversity Officers in Higher Education (NADOHE), Student Affairs Professionals in Higher Education (NASPA), and College Student Educators International (ACPA). He currently serves as a member of the National Advisory Council for the National Conference on Race and Ethnicity (NCORE), and he is the co-chair of the Maryland Community College Diversity Roundtable.

Felton earned a bachelor's degree in psychology and a master's degree in educational administration from McDaniel College in Westminster, Maryland. He is currently pursuing his doctorate in global leadership with a concentration in academic administration from Indiana Tech in Fort Wayne, Indiana.